# A GUIDE TO THE CIV DISTRICTS OF CHES

## Introduction

This Guide is designed as an aid to researching the local records of civil registration in Cheshire. Since the registration of births, marriages and deaths was begun in July 1837, there have been a considerable number of boundary changes, resulting in the transfer of many records to different register offices. Although duplicate copies may be ordered from the General Register Office, it is often more convenient (and less expensive) to purchase certificates from the local Superintendent Registrars.

## Registration Districts in Cheshire

For registration purposes Cheshire was originally divided into nine districts (Stockport, Macclesfield, Altrincham, Runcorn, Northwich, Congleton, Nantwich, Great Boughton and Wirral), based on the boundaries of the Poor-Law Unions set up in 1834. Each district was further divided into between three and seven sub-districts, each maintaining its own sets of registers of births and deaths. For marriages, the situation was a little more complex (see below).

During the nineteenth century there were some changes to the registration districts and sub-districts. In 1861 Birkenhead district was created from part of Wirral district; the Great Boughton district was renamed 'Chester' in 1870, and similarly the Altrincham district was called 'Bucklow' from 1898. A further complication at this time was that small areas of Cheshire were included in registration districts in neighbouring counties, and likewise, small parts of Lancashire, Staffordshire and Flintshire were included in the Stockport, Congleton and Chester districts.

In 1936 and 1937 there were considerable changes to the Cheshire registration service. Congleton district was abolished and divided between Macclesfield and the old Nantwich district, now renamed 'Crewe'. The boundaries of Birkenhead, Chester, Stockport and Wallasey districts were made co-terminous with the County Boroughs in those towns, and new districts were created in West Cheshire, North East Cheshire and Hyde. All the district and sub-districts were altered to take account of local government changes in the period 1931-37, and district boundaries no longer cut across county boundaries.

This scheme remained in effect until 1974, when 'new' Cheshire was created. Large parts of the old county were annexed to Merseyside and Greater Manchester, and the Warrington and Widnes areas of Lancashire were moved to Cheshire. The present system of six registration districts was established (Chester & Ellesmere Port, Congleton & Crewe, Halton, Macclesfield, Vale Royal and Warrington). In 1988 the Congleton & Crewe district was renamed 'South Cheshire'.

## Townships and Civil Parishes (CPs)

In 1837 the smallest units of local government were townships, which were subdivisions of the ancient parishes. Registration districts and sub-districts usually comprised several dozen townships. In the 1850s and 1860s townships were restyled 'Civil Parishes' (as distinct from ecclesiastical parishes), which are still in existence today. To avoid unnecessary confusion, both townships and civil parishes are referred to in the guide by the abbreviation 'CP'.

From the 1880s onwards there were numerous changes to CP boundaries, particularly in 1894 and 1936. Where necessary, the registration districts and sub-districts were altered accordingly, though not always immediately. Sometimes the changes resulted in CPs being divided between two or more districts or sub-districts. All relevant changes are listed in the section 'Registration Districts and Sub-Districts in Cheshire'. More detailed information on local government boundary changes may be found in the printed Census Reports (1901-71), or in Volume 2 of the Victoria County History of Cheshire.

## Locating Registers of Births and Deaths

Births and deaths were supposed to be registered in the sub-districts in which the event took place (though in the first fifty-years or so of civil registration there were many irregularities, with events being registered in neighbouring sub-districts, or not being recorded at all). If you know roughly when and where the birth or death occurred, first look at the Index of Civil Parishes, to find out which district and sub-district the CP belonged to, and then consult the alphabetical list of Registration Districts and Sub-Districts, to see which office currently holds the registers.

## Locating Registers of Marriages

*(a)* If the marriage took place in a Church of England, Jewish, or Society of Friends' (Quaker) place of worship, the records for each church or chapel are kept individually, and should be held in the registration district in which the building is *currently* situated; this can be found from the Index of Civil Parishes.

*(b)* If the marriage took place in any other nonconformist church or chapel before 1898, the records were kept by sub-district, and can be located in the same way as birth and death registers. After 1898 some of the larger nonconformist places of worship were allowed to keep their own registers, and these should have been transferred to the district in which the building is *currently* situated.

*(c)* All marriages by registrar were kept by sub-district, and should be with the registers of births and deaths for the sub-district concerned.

## District Register Offices

Although birth, marriage and death certificates can be issued by local superintendent registrars, there are some restrictions that the researcher should bear in mind. The main priority of district register offices is to record *current* births, deaths and marriages, and the needs of the family historian will inevitably take second place. Visits to register offices may not be convenient on a Monday morning, for example, when many weekend births and deaths are being registered, or on a Friday or Saturday, which are popular times for marriages. Postal applications are normally dealt with within two weeks.

If a reasonable amount of information is provided, registrars will search their indexes for a period of up to five years of the date of any particular birth, death or marriage. A long search can be involved when looking for a marriage if the church or chapel is not known, since most churches kept their own sets of registers, and a register office typically includes records for dozens of churches. For a price, the public themselves are allowed to make a 'general search' of the indexes for up to six hours, though only by prior arrangement with the Superintendent Registrar.

It should be noted that reference numbers obtained from the St. Catherine's House indexes, which cover the whole of England and Wales, are completely useless to a district register office. Boundary changes have also rendered some of the information obsolete: for instance, the national indexes might show that a particular a marriage took place in the Bucklow registration district in 1900, but the local records of this event could now at any one of five different register offices.

**Editor's Note**

I would like to thank the various local Superintendent Registrars who have patiently assisted me in the compilation of this guide, especially Mrs. Harrison and Mrs. O'Neill of Northwich. Although every care has been taken to ensure that the details shown are accurate, in some cases the source information is fragmentary and contradictory, particularly for the nineteenth century. If the reader should come across any certificates which would seem to be at odds with the information in the guide, I would like to hear from them.

B. Langston,

Family History Society of Cheshire.                                       February 1996.

### Key to Abbreviations

| | | | |
|---|---|---|---|
| CP | Civil Parish/Township | *Lancs.* | Lancashire |
| *Ches.* | Cheshire | *Mers.* | Merseyside |
| *Denb.* | Denbighshire | *Salop* | Shropshire |
| *Derb.* | Derbyshire | *Staffs* | Staffordshire |
| *Flint* | Flintshire | | |
| *Gtr. Man.* | Greater Manchester | | |

# REGISTRATION DISTRICTS AND SUB-DISTRICTS IN CHESHIRE (1837–1974)

## ALTRINCHAM DISTRICT
Created 1837 from the CPs in Altrincham Poor-Law Union. Renamed BUCKLOW in 1898 (q.v.).

### Altrincham sub-district (1837–98):
Registers now in TRAFFORD district
1837 July 1st   Created from Altrincham, Ashley, Ashton upon Mersey, Baguley, Bowdon, Dunham Massey, Hale, Sale and Timperley CPs.
1898 October 1st   Abolished (incorporated into BUCKLOW district).

### Knutsford sub-district (1837–98):
Registers now in MACCLESFIELD district.
1837 July 1st   Created from Bexton, Knutsford Nether, Knutsford Over, Marthall cum Warford, Mere, Ollerton, Peover Inferior, Peover Superior, Pickmere, Plumley, Rostherne, Tabley Inferior, Tabley Superior, Tatton and Toft CPs.
1895 April 1st   Knutsford Nether and Knutsford Over CPs were united to create Knutsford CP.
1898 October 1st   Abolished (incorporated into BUCKLOW district).

### Lymm sub-district (1837–98):
Registers now in WARRINGTON district.
1837 July 1st   Created from Agden, Aston by Budworth, Bollington, Carrington, High Legh, Lymm, Millington, Partington and Warburton CPs.
1898 October 1st   Abolished (incorporated into BUCKLOW district).

### Wilmslow sub-district (1837–98):
Registers now in MACCLESFIELD district.
1837 July 1st   Created from Bollin Fee, Fulshaw, Mobberley, Northenden, Northen Etchells and Pownall Fee CPs.
1894 September 30th   *(a)* Wilmslow CP was created from parts of Bollin Fee, Fulshaw and Pownall Fee CPs.
*(b)* The remaining part of Fulshaw CP was added to Bollin Fee CP.
*(c)* The remaining part of Pownall Fee CP was renamed Styal CP.
1898 October 1st   Abolished (incorporated into BUCKLOW district).

## ASHTON UNDER LYNE DISTRICT

Created 1837 from the CPs in Ashton and Oldham Poor-Law Unions (mainly in *Lancs.*). In *Lancs.* Registration County. Prior to 1850 the district was known simply as ASHTON. Abolished 1937, when the CPs in *Ches.* were transferred to HYDE district.

### Dukinfield sub-district (1837-97):
Registers now in TAMESIDE district

| | |
|---|---|
| 1837 July 1st | Created from Dukinfield CP. |
| 1883 January 1st | Extended to include Matley and Stayley CPs and the hamlet of Micklehurst in Tintwistle CP (formerly in Stayley sub-district). |
| 1894 November (?) | (a) Stalybridge CP was extended to include the whole of Stayley CP and part of Dukinfield CP. |
| | (b) The part of Tintwistle CP in Dukinfield sub-district (i.e. the hamlet of Micklehurst) was added to Mossley CP [*Lancs.*]. |
| 1897 April 1st | Abolished (the part in *Ches.* was transferred to Stalybridge sub-district). |

### Dukinfield sub-district (1911-37):
Registers now in TAMESIDE district

| | |
|---|---|
| 1911 April 1st | Created from Dukinfield CP (formerly in Stalybridge sub-district). |
| 1936 April 1st | Dukinfield CP was extended to include parts of Hyde and Matley CPs, but these areas were not added to Dukinfield sub-district. |
| 1937 April 1st | Abolished (incorporated into HYDE district). |

### Hartshead sub-district (partly in *Ches.*, 1894-98):
Registers now in TAMESIDE district

| | |
|---|---|
| 1894 November (?) | Part of Ashton-under-Lyne CP [*Lancs.*] was added to Stalybridge CP (thus becoming part of *Ches.*), but remained in Hartshead sub-district. |
| 1897 April 1st | The part of Stalybridge CP in Hartshead sub-district was transferred to Stalybridge sub-district. |

### Mottram sub-district (1837-1937):
Registers now in TAMESIDE district

| | |
|---|---|
| 1837 July 1st | Created from Hattersley, Hollingworth and Mottram CPs, and Tintwistle CP (except for the hamlet of Micklehurst). |

**Mottram sub-district** *(continued)*

1894 November (?)     The part of Tintwistle CP in Dukinfield sub-district was added to Mossley CP [*Lancs.*]; thus the whole of Tintwistle CP was now in Mottram sub-district.

1936 April 1st     *(a)* The whole of Hollingworth and Mottram CPs and part of Hattersley CP became part of Longendale CP.
    *(b)* The remaining part of Hattersley CP was added to Hyde CP (but remained in Mottram sub-district).

1937 April 1st     Abolished (incorpoated into HYDE district).

**Newton sub-district (1837–1923):**
Registers now in TAMESIDE district.
1837 July 1st     Created from Godley and Newton CPs.
1923 October 1st     Abolished (Godley and Newton CPs were added to Hyde CP and transferred to STOCKPORT district).

**Stalybridge sub-district (1897–1937):**
Registers now in TAMESIDE district
1897 April 1st     Created from Dukinfield, Matley and Stalybridge CPs (formerly in Dukinfield and Hartshead sub-districts).
1898 November 9th     *(a)* Part of Dukinfield CP was added to Ashton-under-Lyne CP (and thus transferred to *Lancs.*)
    *(b)* Part of Ashton-under-Lyne CP [*Lancs.*] was added to Dukinfield CP (and thus transferred to *Ches.*).
1911 August 1st     Dukinfield CP was transferred to Dukinfield sub-district.
1936 April 1st     Matley CP was abolished and incorporated into Dukinfield, Hyde and Longendale CPs (but the area remained in Stalybridge sub-district).
1937 April 1st     Abolished (incorporated into HYDE district).

**Stayley sub-district (1837–82):**
Registers now in TAMESIDE district
1837 July 1st     Created from Matley and Stayley CPs, and the hamlet of Micklehurst in Tintwistle CP.
1883 January 1st     Abolished (incorporated into Dukinfield sub-district).

## BIRKENHEAD DISTRICT

Created 1861 out of the CPs in Birkenhead Poor-Law Union (formerly part of WIRRAL district). From 1937 to 1974 the district comprised the area of Birkenhead County Borough. Since 1974 the area has been part of *Mers*.

**Birkenhead sub-district (1861–1937):**
Registers now in BIRKENHEAD district.
1861 August 1st             Created from Birkenhead CP (formerly in WIRRAL district).
1898 March 31st             Birkenhead CP was extended to include parts of other CPs, but these areas were not added to Birkenhead sub-district.
1937 April 1st              Abolished (incorporated into Birkenhead North sub-district).

**Birkenhead North sub-district (1937–74):**
Registers now in BIRKENHEAD district.
1937 April 1st              Created from the part of Birkenhead CP in the Argyle, Cathcart, Cleveland, Gilbrook, Grange, St. James and Upton wards of Birkenhead County Borough.
1974 April 1st              Abolished (Birkenhead CP was transferred to *Mers.*).

**Birkenhead South sub-district (1937–74):**
Registers now in BIRKENHEAD district.
1937 April 1st              Created from the part of Birkenhead CP in the Bebington, Claughton, Clifton, Devonshire, Egerton, Holt, Mersey, Oxton and Prenton wards of Birkenhead County Borough.
1974 April 1st              Abolished (Birkenhead CP was transferred to *Mers.*).

**Tranmere sub-district (1861–1937):**
Registers now in BIRKENHEAD district.
1861 August 1st             Created from Bidston cum Ford, Claughton cum Grange, Noctorum, Oxton and Tranmere CPs (formerly in WIRRAL district).
1898 March 31st             *(a)* Birkenhead sub-district and Birkenhead CP were extended to include the whole of Rock Ferry CP and part of Lower Bebington CP (formerly in WIRRAL district).
                            *(b)* Claughton cum Grange, Oxton and Tranmere CPs were abolished and added to Birkenhead CP, but these areas remained in Tranmere sub-district.
1928 April 1st              Part of Bidston cum Ford CP was added to Wallasey CP, but remained in Tranmere sub-district.
1933 April 1st              *(a)* Bidston cum Ford CP was abolished and incorporated into Birkenhead and Wallasey CPs, but the area remained wholly in Tranmere sub-district.
                            *(b)* Noctorum CP was abolished and added to Birkenhead CP, but the area remained in Tranmere sub-district.
1936 April 1st              The part of Wallasey CP in Tranmere sub-district (which had formerly been part of Bidston cum Ford CP) was transferred to WALLASEY district.
1937 April 1st              Abolished (incorporated into Birkenhead South sub-district).

**Wallasey sub-district (1861–1936):**
Registers now in WALLASEY district.
| | |
|---|---|
| 1861 August 1st | Created from Liscard, Poulton cum Seacombe and Wallasey CPs (formerly in WIRRAL district). |
| 1912 April 1st | Wallasey CP was extended to include the whole of Liscard and Poulton cum Seacombe CPs (thus Wallasey sub-district became co-extensive with Wallasey CP). |
| 1928 April 1st | (a) Wallasey sub-district and Wallasey CP were extended to include the whole of Moreton CP (formerly in WIRRAL district) |
| | (b) Wallasey CP was extended to include part of Bidston cum Ford, but this area remained in Tranmere sub-district. |
| 1933 April 1st | Wallasey sub-district and Wallasey CP were extended to include parts of Saughall Massie and Upton by Birkenhead CPs (formerly in WIRRAL district). |
| 1936 April 1st | Abolished (incorporated into WALLASEY district). |

## BUCKLOW DISTRICT

Created 1898 by renaming of ALTRINCHAM district. Abolished 1974, and divided between MACCLESFIELD, WARRINGTON districts [Ches.], and MANCHESTER, TRAFFORD districts [Gtr. Man.].

**Altrincham sub-district (1898–1974):**
Registers now in TRAFFORD district.
| | |
|---|---|
| 1898 October 1st | Created from Altrincham, Ashley, Ashton upon Mersey, Baguley, Bowdon, Dunham Massey, Hale, Sale and Timperley CPs. |
| 1900 April 1st | Ringway CP was created from part of Hale CP. |
| 1903 April 1st | Ashton upon Mersey, Baguley and Sale CPs were transferred to Sale sub-district. |
| 1920 October 1st | Altrincham sub-district and Altrincham CP were extended to include part of Carrington CP (formerly in Sale sub-district). |
| 1936 April 1st | Timperley CP was abolished and divided between Altrincham and Hale CPs. |
| 1974 April 1st | Abolished (Altrincham, Bowdon, Dunham Massey and Hale CPs were transferred to TRAFFORD district; Ashley CP was transferred to MACCLESFIELD district; Ringway CP was transferred to MANCHESTER district). |

## Knutsford sub-district (1898–1974):
Registers now in MACCLESFIELD district.

| | |
|---|---|
| 1898 October 1st | Created from Bexton, Knutsford, Marthall cum Warford, Mere, Ollerton, Peover Inferior, Peover Superior, Pickmere, Plumley, Rostherne, Tabley Inferior, Tabley Superior, Tatton and Toft CPs. |
| 1936 April 1st | *(a)* Part of Pickmere CP was added to Wincham CP, but the area remained in Knutsford sub-district.<br>*(b)* Tabley Inferior CP was extended to include part of Wincham CP, but this area was not added to Knutsford sub-district. |
| 1937 April 1st | *(a)* Extended to include Agden, Aston by Budworth, Bollington, High Legh, Lymm, Millington, Mobberley, Partington and Warburton CPs (formerly in Lymm and Wilmslow sub-districts)<br>*(b)* Extended to include the part of Tabley Inferior CP in NORTHWICH district (which until 1936 had been part of Wincham CP).<br>*(c)* The part of Pickmere CP (which until 1936 had been part of Wincham CP) was transfered to NORTHWICH district. |
| 1951 April 1st | Marthall cum Warford CP was abolished, and divided between Marthall CP and Little Warford CP. |
| 1962 April 1st | Agden, Carrington, High Legh, Lymm, Partington and Warburton CPs were transferred to Lymm sub-district. |
| 1974 April 1st | Abolished (incorporated into MACCLESFIELD district). |

## Lymm sub-district (1898–1937):
Registers now in WARRINGTON district.

| | |
|---|---|
| 1898 October 1st | Created from Agden, Aston by Budworth, Bollington, Carrington, High Legh, Lymm, Millington, Partington and Warburton CPs. |
| 1903 April 1st | Carrington CP was transferred to Sale sub-district. |
| 1920 April 1st | The county boundary between Partington and Warburton CPs [*Ches.*] and Irlam and Rixton-with-Glazebrook CPs [*Lancs.*], was altered to follow the Manchester Ship Canal. |
| 1920 October 1st | The boundary between Lymm sub-district and BARTON-UPON-IRWELL district was adjusted to take account of the changes on 1st April 1920. |
| 1933 April 1st | The county boundary between Lymm and Warburton CPs [*Ches.*] and Rixton-with-Glazebrook and Woolston-with-Martinscroft CPs [*Lancs.*] was altered to follow the Manchester Ship Canal (without changing the boundary of Lymm sub-district). |
| 1937 April 1st | Abolished (incorporated into Knutsford sub-district). |

**Lymm sub-district (1962–74):**
Registers now in WARRINGTON district.
| | |
|---|---|
| 1962 April 1st | Created from Agden, Carrington, High Legh, Lymm, Partington and Warburton CPs (formerly in Knutsford and Sale sub-districts). |
| 1974 April 1st | Abolished (Agden CP was transferred to MACCLESFIELD district; High Legh and Lymm CPs to WARRINGTON district; Carrington, Partington and Warburton CPs to TRAFFORD district). |

**Sale sub-district (1903–74):**
Registers now in TRAFFORD district.
| | |
|---|---|
| 1903 April 1st | Created from Ashton upon Mersey, Baguley, Carrington, Northenden and Sale CPs (formerly in Altrincham, Lymm and Wilmslow sub-districts). |
| 1920 April 1st | The county boundary between Carrington CP [*Ches.*] and Flixton and Irlam CPs [*Lancs.*] was altered to follow the Manchester Ship Canal. |
| 1920 October 1st | *(a)* The boundary between Sale sub-district and BARTON-UPON-IRWELL district was altered to take account of the changes on 1st April 1920. |
| | *(b)* Part of Carrington CP was added to Altrincham CP and transferred to Altrincham sub-district. |
| 1931 April 1st | Baguley and Northenden CPs were abolished and added to Manchester CP [*Lancs.*], but these areas remained within Sale sub-district. |
| 1936 April 1st | *(a)* The part of Manchester CP (which formerly comprised Baguley and Northenden CPs) was transferred to SOUTH MANCHESTER district. |
| | *(b)* Ashton-upon Mersey CP was abolished and added to Sale CP. |
| 1974 April 1st | Abolished. (incorporated into TRAFFORD district). |

**Wilmslow sub-district (1898–1974):**
Registers now in MACCLESFIELD district.
| | |
|---|---|
| 1898 October 1st | Created from Bollin Fee, Mobberley, Northenden, Northen Etchells, Styal and Wilmslow CPs. |
| 1931 April 1st | Northen Etchells CP was abolished and added to Manchester CP [*Lancs.*], but the area remained within Wilmslow sub-district. |
| 1936 April 1st | *(a)* The part of Manchester CP (which formerly comprised Northen Etchells CP) was transferred to SOUTH MANCHESTER district |

**Wilmslow sub-district** *(continued)*

1936 April 1st      *(b)* Bollin Fee CP was abolished and added to Alderley Edge CP, but the area remained in Wilmslow sub-district.

*(c)* Styal CP was abolished and added to Wilmslow CP.

1937 April 1st      *(a)* Extended to include the part of Alderley Edge CP in MACCLESFIELD district.

*(b)* Mobberley CP was transferred to Knutsford sub-district.

1974 April 1st      Abolished (incorporated into MACCLESFIELD district).


## CHESTER DISTRICT

Created 1870 by the renaming of GREAT BOUGHTON district. From 1937 to 1974 the district comprised the area in Chester County Borough. Abolished 1974 and incorporated into CHESTER & ELLESMERE PORT district.

**Chester sub-district (1937–74):**
Registers now in CHESTER & ELLESMERE PORT district.

1937 April 1st      Created from Chester CP.

1954 April 1st      Chester sub-district and Chester CP were extended to include parts of Hoole and Upton by Chester CPs (formerly in WEST CHESHIRE district).

1974 April 1st      Abolished (incorporated into CHESTER & ELLESMERE PORT district).

**Chester Castle sub-district (1870–1918):**
Registers now in CHESTER & ELLESMERE PORT district.

1870 January 1st      Created from Chester Castle, St. John the Baptist, St. Mary on the Hill, St. Michael, St. Olave and Spital Boughton CPs.

1871 August 1st      Extended to include Christleton, Claverton, Dodleston, Eaton, Eccleston, Great Boughton, Littleton, Lower Kinnerton, Marlston cum Lache, Poulton and Pulford CPs (formerly in Great Boughton and Hawarden sub-districts).

1884 March (?)      St. John the Baptist, St. Mary on the Hill, St. Michael, St. Olave and Spital Boughton CPs were abolished and incorporated into Chester CP.

1908 (?)      Queen's Park (a detached part of Chester Castle sub-district south of the River Dee) was transferred to Chester Cathedral sub-district.

1918 July 1st      Abolished (incorporated into Chester City and Chester Rural sub-districts).

**Chester Cathedral sub-district (1870–1918):**
Registers now in CHESTER & ELLESMERE PORT district.
1870 January 1st          Created from Cathedral Precincts, Holy Trinity, St. Bridget, St. Martin, St. Oswald and St. Peter CPs.
1871 August 1st           Extended to include Bache, Backford, Blacon cum Crabwall, Bridge Trafford, Capenhurst, Caughall, Chorlton by Backford, Croughton, Dunham on the Hill, Elton, Great Mollington, Great Saughall, Great Stanney, Hapsford, Hoole, Ince, Lea by Backford, Little Mollington, Little Saughall, Little Stanney, Mickle Trafford, Moston, Newton by Chester, Picton, Shotwick, Shotwick Park, Stanlow, Stoke, Thornton le Moors, Upton by Chester, Wervin, Wimbolds Trafford and Woodbank CPs (formerly in Great Boughton and Hawarden sub-districts).
1884 March (?)            Cathedral Precincts, Holy Trinity, St. Bridget, St. Martin, St. Oswald and St. Peter CPs were abolished and incorporated into Chester CP.
1894 Sepember (?)         Hoole Village CP was created from part of Hoole CP.
1901 March 25th           Great Mollington and Little Mollington CPs were united to create Mollington CP.
1908 (?)                  Extended to include Queen's Park (formerly a detached part of Chester Castle sub-district south of the River Dee).
1918 July 1st             Abolished (incorporated into Chester City and Chester Rural sub-districts).

**Chester City sub-district (1918–37):**
Registers now in CHESTER & ELLESMERE PORT district.
1918 July 1st             Created from the whole of Chester CP (formerly in Chester Castle and Chester Cathedral sub-districts).
1936 April 1st            Chester CP was extended to include parts of other CPs, but these areas were not added to Chester City sub-district.
1937 April 1st            Abolished (incorporated into Chester sub-district).

**Chester Rural sub-district (1918–37):**
Registers now in CHESTER & ELLESMERE PORT district.
1918 April 1st            Created from Bache, Backford, Blacon cum Crabwall, Bridge Trafford, Capenhurst, Caughall, Chester Castle, Chorlton by Backford, Christleton, Claverton, Croughton, Dodleston, Dunham on the Hill, Eaton, Eccleston, Elton, Great Boughton, Great Saughall, Great Stanney, Hapsford, Hoole, Hoole Village, Ince, Lea by Backford, Little Saughall, Little Stanney, Littleton, Lower Kinnerton, Marlston cum Lache, Mickle Trafford, Mollington, Moston, Newton by Chester,

**Chester Rural sub-district** *(continued)*

1918 April 1st  Picton, Poulton, Pulford, Shotwick, Shotwick Park, Stoke, Tarvin, Thornton le Moors, Upton by Chester, Wervin, Wimbolds Trafford and Woodbank CPs (formerly in Chester Castle and Chester Rural sub-districts).

1937 April 1st  Abolished (incorporated into WEST CHESHIRE district).

## Great Boughton sub-district (1870–71):
Registers now in CHESTER & ELLESMERE PORT district.

1870 January 1st  Created from Ashton, Bache, Backford, Barrow, Blacon cum Crabwall, Bridge Trafford, Capenhurst, Caughall, Chorlton by Backford, Christleton, Cotton Abbotts, Cotton Edmunds, Croughton, Dunham on the Hill, Elton, Great Boughton, Great Mollington, Great Stanney, Guilden Sutton, Hapsford, Hockenhull, Hoole, Horton cum Peel, Huntington, Ince, Kelsall, Lea by Backford, Little Mollington, Little Stanney, Littleton, Mickle Trafford, Moston, Mouldsworth, Newton by Chester, Picton, Prior's Heys, Rowton, Stanlow, Stoke, Tarvin, Thornton le Moors, Upton by Chester, Wervin and Wimbolds Trafford CPs.

1871 August 1st  Abolished (incorporated into Chester Castle, Chester Cathedral and Tattenhall sub-districts).

## Hawarden sub-district (1870–1902) [entirely in *Flint*, 1871–1902]
Registers now in ALYN & DEESIDE district.

1870 January 1st  Created from Claverton, Dodleston, Eaton, Eccleston, Great Saughall, Hawarden [*Flint*], Higher Kinnerton [*Flint*], Little Saughall, Lower Kinnerton, Marlston cum Lache, Poulton, Pulford, Saltney [*Flint*], Shotwick, Shotwick Park and Woodbank CPs.

1871 August 1st  *(a)* Extended to include Hope, Merford and Hoseley and Tryddyn CPs (formerly in WREXHAM district)

*(b)* Claverton, Dodles ton, Eaton, Eccleston, Lower Kinnerton, Marlston cum Lache, Poulton and Pulford CPs were transferred to Chester Castle sub-district

*(c)* Great Saughall, Little Saughall, Shotwick, Shotwick Park and Woodbank CPs were transferred to Chester Cathedral sub-district.

1894 September (?)  Sealand CP was created from part of Hawarden CP.

1897 October 1st  Buckley (Hawarden) CP was created from part of Hawarden CP.

1903 January 1st  Abolished (incorporated into HAWARDEN district).

**Tattenhall sub-district (1870–1937):**
Registers now in CHESTER & ELLESMERE PORT district.

| | |
|---|---|
| 1870 January 1st | Created from Aldersey, Aldford, Barton, Broxton, Bruen Stapleford, Buerton, Burton by Tarvin, Caldecott, Carden, Chowley, Churton by Aldford, Churton by Farndon, Churton Heath, Clotton Hoofield, Clutton, Coddington, Crewe by Farndon, Duddon, Edgerley, Farndon, Foulk Stapleford, Golborne Bellow, Golborne David, Grafton, Guilden Sutton, Handley, Harthill, Hatton, Horton, Huxley, Iddinshall, Kelsall, King's Marsh, Lea Newbold, Newton by Tattenhall, Saighton, Stretton, Tattenhall, Tilston, Waverton and Willington CPs. |
| 1871 August 1st | Extended to include Ashton, Barrow, Cotton Abbotts, Cotton Edmunds, Hockenhull, Horton cum Peel, Huntington, Kelsall, Mouldsworth, Prior's Heys, Rowton and Tarvin CPs (formerly in Great Boughton sub-district). |
| 1892 July 1st | Extended to include Beeston, Burwardsley, Eaton, Rushton, Tarporley, Tilstone Fearnall, Tiverton and Utkinton CPs (formerly in NANTWICH district). |
| 1897 January 1st | Extended to include Church Shocklach and Shocklach Oviatt CPs (formerly in WREXHAM district). |
| 1936 April 1st | Part of Tilstone Fearnall CP was added to Bunbury CP, but remained in Tattenhall sub-district. |
| 1937 April 1st | Abolished (incorporated into WEST CHESHIRE, NANTWICH and NORTHWICH districts). |

## CONGLETON DISTRICT

Created 1837 out of the CPs in Congleton Poor-Law Union (in *Ches.* and *Staffs.*).
Abolished 1937, and incorporated into CREWE and MACCLESFIELD districts.

**Church Hulme sub-district (1837–1937):**
Registers now in SOUTH CHESHIRE district.

| | |
|---|---|
| 1837 July 1st | Created from Blackden, Brereton cum Smethwick, Church Hulme, Cotton, Cranage, Davenport, Kermincham, Leese, Swettenham and Twemlow CPs. |
| 1867 July 1st | Extended to include Goostrey cum Barnshaw CP (formerly in NORTHWICH district). |
| 1889 March 24th | Church Hulme sub-district and Twemlow CP were extended to include No Town Farm, a detached part of Rudheath CP (formerly in NORTHWICH district). |

**Church Hulme sub-district** *(continued)*

1936 April 1st
    *(a)* Brereton cum Smethwick and Davenport CPs were united to create Brereton CP.
    *(b)* Cotton CP was abolished and added to Cranage CP.
    *(c)* Part of Cranage CP was added to Lach Dennis CP, but this area remained in Church Hulme sub-district.
    *(d)* Blackden and Goostrey cum Barnshaw CPs were united to create Goostrey CP.
    *(e)* Kermincham CP was abolished and added to Swettenham CP.
    *(f)* Leese CP was abolished and incorporated into Byley, Cranage and Lach Dennis CPs but the area remained wholly in Church Hulme sub-district.

1937 April 1st      Abolished (incorporated into CREWE district).

## Congleton sub-district (1837–1937):
Registers now in SOUTH CHESHIRE district.

1837 July 1st      Created from Biddulph [*Staffs.*], Buglawton, Congleton, Hulme Walfield, Newbold Astbury, Radnor, Somerford and Somerford Booths CPs.

1893 April 1st      Biddulph CP [*Staffs.*] was transferred to LEEK district.

1895 October 1st      Radnor CP was abolished and added to Somerford CP.

1936 April 1st
    *(a)* Buglawton CP was abolished and incorporated into Congleton, Eaton and North Rode CPs, but the area remained wholly in Congleton sub-district.
    *(b)* Congleton CP was extended to include parts of Bosley, Eaton and North Rode CPs, but these areas were not added to Congleton sub-district.

1937 April 1st      Abolished (Moreton cum Alcumlow CP was transferred to CREWE district, and the remaining CPs to MACCLESFIELD district).

## Sandbach sub-district (1837–1937):
Registers now in SOUTH CHESHIRE district.

1837 July 1st      Created from Alsager, Arclid, Betchton, Bradwall, Church Lawton, Elton, Hassall, Moston, Odd Rode, Sandbach, Smallwood, Tetton and Wheelock CPs.

1936 April 1st
    *(a)* Bradwall CP was extended to include a detached part of Kinderton CP (i.e. Higher Daleacre), but this area remained in NORTHWICH district.
    *(b)* Wheelock CP was abolished and incorporated into Haslington and Sandbach CPs, but the area remained wholly in Sandbach sub district.

**Sandbach sub-district** *(continued)*
1936 April 1st  *(c)* Moston CP was abolished and added to Tetton CP
1937 April 1st  Abolished (incorporated into CREWE district).


## CREWE DISTRICT
Created 1937 from parts of CONGLETON, NANTWICH and WHITCHURCH districts. Abolished 1974, and incorporated into CONGLETON & CREWE district.

### Crewe sub-district (1937-74):
Registers now in SOUTH CHESHIRE district.
1937 April 1st  Created from Barthomley, Basford, Crewe, Haslington, Leighton, Minshull Vernon, Monks Coppenhall, Shavington cum Gresty, Warmingham, Weston, Wistaston and Woolstanwood CPs.
1965 April 1st  The county boundary between Weston CP [*Ches.*] and Balterley CP [*Staffs.*] was altered, and the boundary between Crewe sub-district and NEWCASTLE UNDER LYME district was adjusted accordingly.
1974 April 1st  Abolished (transferred to CONGLETON & CREWE district).

### Nantwich sub-district (1937-74):
Registers now in SOUTH CHESHIRE district.
1937 April 1st  Created from Acton, Alpraham, Aston juxta Mondrum, Audlem, Austerson, Baddiley, Baddington, Batherton, Bickerton, Blakenhall, Bridgemere, Brindley, Broomhall, Buerton, Bulkeley, Bunbury, Burland, Calveley, Checkley cum Wrinehill, Cholmondeley, Cholmondeston, Chorley, Chorlton, Church Minshull, Coole Pilate, Dodcott cum Wilkesley, Doddington, Edleston, Egerton, Faddiley, Hankelow, Hatherton, Haughton, Henhull, Hough, Hunsterson, Hurleston, Lea, Marbury cum Quoisley, Nantwich, Newhall, Norbury, Peckforton, Poole, Ridley, Rope, Sound, Spurstow, Stapeley, Stoke, Walgherton, Wardle, Wettenhall, Willaston, Wirswall, Woodcott, Worleston, Wrenbury cum Frith and Wybunbury CPs.
1965 April 1st  The county boundary between Blakenhall, Checkley cum Wrinehill, Chorlton and Marbury cum Quoisley CPs [*Ches.*], Balterley and Betley CPs [*Staffs.*] and Whitchurch CP [*Salop*] was altered, and the boundary between Nantwich sub-district and NEWCASTLE UNDER LYME and WHITCHURCH districts was altered accordingly.
1974 April 1st  Abolished (transferred to CONGLETON & CREWE district).

**Sandbach sub-district (1937-74):**
Registers now in SOUTH CHESHIRE district.
1937 April 1st        Created from Alsager, Arclid, Betchton, Bradwall, Brereton, Church Hulme, Church Lawton, Cranage, Elton, Goostrey, Hassall, Moreton cum Alcumlow, Odd Rode, Sandbach, Smallwood, Swettenham, Tetton and Twemlow CPs.
1965 April 1st        The county boundary between Church Lawton and Odd Rode CPs [*Ches.*] and Kidsgrove and Stoke on Trent CPs [*Staffs.*] was altered, and the boundary between Nantwich sub-district and NEWCASTLE UNDER LYME and STOKE-ON-TRENT districts was adjusted accordingly.
1970 April 1st        Elton and Tetton CPs werw united to create Moston CP.
1974 April 1st        Abolished; (transferred to CONGLETON & CREWE district).


## GLOSSOP DISTRICT
In *Derb*. Registration County.

**Glossop sub-district (partly in *Ches*. 1936-37):**
Registers now in HIGH PEAK district.
1936 April 1st        Mellor CP [*Derb.*] was abolished and added to Marple CP [*Ches.*], but the area remained in Glossop sub-district.
1937 April 1st        Abolished (the part in *Ches*. was transferred to NORTH EAST CHESHIRE district).


## GREAT BOUGHTON DISTRICT
Created 1837 out of the CPs in Great Boughton, Hawarden and Tarvin Poor-Law Unions and the City of Chester. Renamed CHESTER in 1870 (q.v.).

**Chester Castle Division sub-district (1837-69):**
Registers now in CHESTER & ELLESMERE PORT district.
1837 July 1st         Created from Ashton, Barrow, Chester Castle, Christleton, Cotton Abbotts, Cotton Edmunds, Great Boughton, Guilden Sutton, Hockenhull, Horton cum Peel, Huntington, Kelsall, Littleton, Mouldsworth, Prior's Heys, Rowton, St. John the Baptist, St. Mary on the Hill, St. Michael, St. Olave, Spital Boughton and Tarvin CPs.
1870 January 1st      Abolished (incorporated into CHESTER district).

**Chester Cathedral Division sub-district (1837-69):**
Registers now in CHESTER & ELLESMERE PORT district.
1837 July 1st         Created from Bache, Backford, Blacon cum Crabwall, Bridge Trafford, Capenhurst, Cathedral Precincts, Caughall, Chorlton by Backford, Croughton, Dunham on the Hill, Elton, Great Mollington, Great Stanney, Hapsford, Holy Trinity, Hoole, Ince, Lea by Backford, Little Mollington, Little Stanney, Mickle Trafford, Moston, Newton by Chester, Picton, St. Bridget, St. Martin, St. Oswald, St. Peter, Stanlow, Stoke, Thornton le Moors, Upton by Chester, Wervin and Wimbolds Trafford CPs.
1870 January 1st      Abolished (incorporated into CHESTER district).

**Hawarden sub-district (1837-69):**
Registers now in CHESTER & ELLESMERE PORT district.
1837 July 1st         Created from Aston [*Flint*], Bannel [*Flint*], Bretton [*Flint*], Broad Lane [*Flint*], Broughton [*Flint*], Claverton, Dodleston, Eaton, Eccleston, Ewloe Town [*Flint*], Ewloe Wood [*Flint*], Great Saughall, Hawarden [*Flint*], Higher Kinnerton [*Flint*], Little Saughall, Lower Kinnerton, Manor & Rake [*Flint*], Mancott [*Flint*], Marlston cum Lache, Moor [*Flint*], Pentrobbin [*Flint*], Poulton, Pulford, Saltney [*Flint*], Sealand [*Flint*], Shotton [*Flint*], Shotwick, Shotwick Park and Woodbank CPs.
1870 January 1st      Abolished (incorporated into CHESTER district).

**Tattenhall sub-district (1837-69):**
Registers now in CHESTER & ELLESMERE PORT district.
1837 July 1st         Created from Aldersey, Aldford, Barton, Broxton, Bruen Stapleford, Buerton, Burton by Tarvin, Caldecott, Carden, Chowley, Churton by Aldford, Churton by Farndon, Churton Heath, Clotton Hoofield, Clutton, Coddington, Crewe by Farndon, Duckington, Duddon, Edge, Edgerley, Farndon, Foulk Stapleford, Golborne Bellow, Golborne David, Grafton, Handley, Harthill, Hatton, Horton, Huxley, Iddinshall, King's Marsh, Lea Newbold, Newton by Tattenhall, Saighton, Stretton, Tattenhall, Tilston, Waverton and Willington CPs.
1853 April 1st        Duckington and Edge CPs were transferred to WHITCHURCH district.
1870 January 1st      Abolished (incorporated into CHESTER district).

## HAYFIELD DISTRICT
Created 1837 out of the CPs in Glossop and Hayfield Poor-Law Unions (mainly in *Derb.*). In *Derb.* Registration County. Prior to 1850 the district was named HAYFIELD & GLOSSOP. Abolished 1937, when the part in *Ches.* was transferred to NORTH EAST CHESHIRE district.

### Hayfield sub-district (1837-1937):
Registers now in HIGH PEAK district.

| | |
|---|---|
| 1837 July 1st | Created, including Disley CP in *Ches.* (the remaining CPs were in *Derb.*). |
| 1894 September (?) | Newtown CP was created from part of Disley CP, and transferred to *Derb.* |
| 1936 April 1st | (a) The county boundary between Disley CP [*Ches.*] and New Mills and Whaley Bridge CPs [*Derb.*] was altered, without changing the boundary of Hayfield sub-districts |
| | (b) Disley CP was extended to include part of Yeardsley cum Whaley CP, but this area remained in Macclesfield sub-district. |
| | (c) Ludworth CP [*Derb.*] was abolished and added to Marple CP [*Ches.*], but remained in Hayfield sub-district. |
| 1937 April 1st | Abolished (the part in *Ches.* was transferred to NORTH EAST CHESHIRE district). |

## HYDE DISTRICT
Created 1937 from parts of ASHTON UNDER LYNE and STOCKPORT districts. Abolished 1974 and incorporated into TAMESIDE and HIGH PEAK districts.

### Dukinfield sub-district (1937-69):
Registers now in TAMESIDE district.

| | |
|---|---|
| 1937 April 1st | Created from Dukinfield CP. |
| 1969 April 1st | Abolished (incorporated into Dukinfield & Stalybridge sub-district). |

### Dukinfield & Stalybridge sub-district (1969-74):
Registers now in TAMESIDE district.

| | |
|---|---|
| 1969 April 1st | Created from Dukinfield, Longendale, Stalybridge and Tintwistle CPs (formerly in Stalybridge and Dukinfield sub-districts). |
| 1974 April 1st | Abolished (Dukinfield, Longendale and Stalybridge CPs were transferred to TAMESIDE district, and Tintwistle CP to HIGH PEAK). |

**Hyde sub-district (1937-74):**
Registers now in TAMESIDE district.
1937 April 1st         Created from Hyde CP.
1969 April 1st         Abolished (incorporated into TAMESIDE district).

**Stalybridge sub-district (1937-69):**
Registers now in TAMESIDE district.
1937 April 1st         Created from Longendale, Stalybridge and Tintwistle CPs.
1969 April 1st         Abolished (incorporated into Dukinfield & Stalybridge sub-district).


# MACCLESFIELD DISTRICT
Created 1837 from the CPs in Macclesfield Poor-Law Union.

**Alderley sub-district (1837-1937):**
Registers now in MACCLESFIELD district.
1837 July 1st         Created from Birtles, Capesthorne, Chelford, Chorley, Great Warford, Lower Withington, Nether Alderley, Old Withington, Over Alderley and Snelson CPs.
1893 September 30th  Alderley Edge CP was created from part of Chorley CP.
1936 April 1st         The following changes to CPs took place without alteration to the boundary of the sub-district:
                              *(a)* Birtles CP was abolished and added to Henbury CP.
                              *(b)* Capesthorne CP was abolished and added to Siddington CP.
                              *(c)* Part of Great Warford CP was added to Mobberley CP.
                              *(d)* Lower Withington and Old Withington CPs were united to create Withington CP.
1937 April 1st         Abolished (incorporated into Macclesfield sub-district).

**Bollington sub-district (1837-1937):**
Registers now in MACCLESFIELD district.
1837 July 1st         Created from Bollington, Hurdsfield, Lyme Handley, Pott Shrigley and Tytherington CPs.
1894 September 30th  Part of Hurdsfield CP was added to Macclesfield CP and transferred to East Macclesfield sub-district.
1894 September (?)  Kerridge CP was created from part of Bollington CP.
1900 September 30th  Kerridge CP was abolished and added to Bollington CP.
1928 April 1st         Extended to include Kettleshulme, Rainow, Taxal and Yeardsley cum Whaley CPs (formerly in Rainow sub-district).

**Bollington sub-district** *(continued)*

1936 April 1st   The following changes to CPs took place, without alteration to the boundary of the sub-district:
   *(a)* Bollington CP was extended to include parts of Adlington and Butley CPs.
   *(b)* Part of Hurdsfield CP was added to Macclesfield CP.
   *(c)* Part of Kettleshulme CP was added to Whaley Bridge CP [*Derb.*].
   *(d)* Taxal CP was abolished, and incorporated into Hartington Upper Quarter CP [*Derb.*], Whaley Bridge CP [*Derb.*] and Wildboarclough CP [*Ches.*].
   *(e)* Tytherington CP was abolished, and incorporated into Bollington and Macclesfield CPs.
   *(f)* Yeardsley cum Whaley CP were abolished and incorporated into Disley CP [*Ches.*] and Whaley Bridge CP [*Derb.*].

1937 April 1st   Abolished (the parts in *Ches.* were transferred to Macclesfield sub-district).

**Congleton sub-district (1937–74):**
Registers now in SOUTH CHESHIRE district.

1937 April 1st   Created from Congleton, Hulme Walfield, Newbold Astbury, Somerford and Somerford Booths CPs (formerly in CONGLETON district).

1974 April 1st   Abolished (transferred to CONGLETON & CREWE district).

**East Macclesfield sub-district (1837–1907):**
Registers now in MACCLESFIELD district.

1837 July 1st   Created from the part of Macclesfield CP on the east side of the Leek to Stockport turnpike road.

1894 September 30th   East Macclesfield sub-district and Macclesfield CP were extended to include part of Hurdsfield CP (formerly in Bollington sub-district).

1907 April 1st   Abolished (incorporated into Macclesfield sub-district).

**Gawsworth sub-district (1837–1937):**
Registers now in MACCLESFIELD district.

1837 July 1st   Created from Bosley, Eaton, Gawsworth, Henbury cum Pexall, Marton, North Rode and Siddington CPs.

1910 December 1st   Extended to include Sutton, Wildboarclough and Wincle CPs (formerly in Sutton sub-district).

1928 April 1st   Extended to include Macclesfield Forest CP (formerly in Rainow sub-district).

**Gawsworth sub-district** *(continued)*

| | |
|---|---|
| 1936 April 1st | The following changes to CPs took place, without alteration to the boundary of the sub-district:<br>(a) Parts of Bosley, Eaton and North Rode CPs were added to Congleton CP.<br>(b) Parts of Buglawton CP were added to Eaton and North Rode CPs.<br>(c) Parts of Gawsworth and Sutton CPs were added to Macclesfield CP.<br>(d) Henbury cum Pexall CP was abolished and added to Henbury CP.<br>(e) Capesthorne CP was abolished and added to Siddington CP.<br>(f) Part of Taxal CP was added to Wildboarclough CP. |
| 1937 April 1st | Abolished (incorporated mainly into Macclesfield sub-district). |

**Macclesfield sub-district (1907–48):**
Registers now in MACCLESFIELD district.

| | |
|---|---|
| 1907 April 1st | Created from Macclesfield CP (formerly part of East Macclesfield, Sutton and West Macclesfield sub-districts). |
| 1936 April 1st | Macclesfield CP was extended to include parts of neighbouring CPs, and part of Macclesfield CP was added to Henbury CP (without changing the boundary of Macclesfield sub-district). |
| 1937 April 1st | Extended to include Adlington, Bollington, Bosley, Chelford, Chorley, Eaton, Gawsworth, Great Warford, Henbury, Hurdsfield, Kettleshulme, Lyme Handley, Macclesfield Forest, Marton, Mottram St. Andrew, Nether Alderley, North Rode, Over Alderley, Pott Shrigley, Poynton with Worth, Prestbury, Rainow, Siddington, Snelson, Sutton, Wildboarclough, Wincle, Withington, and Woodford CPs. |
| 1939 April 1st | Woodford CP was transferred to NORTH EAST CHESHIRE district and added to Hazel Grove cum Bramhall CP. |
| 1948 October 1st | Abolished (Bollington and Macclesfield CPs were transferred to Macclesfield & Bollington sub-district, and the other CPs to Macclesfield Rural sub-district). |

**Macclesfield & Bollington sub-district (1948–74):**
Registers now in MACCLESFIELD district.

| | |
|---|---|
| 1948 October 1st | Created from Bollington and Macclesfield CPs (formerly in Macclesfield sub-district). |
| 1955 March 8th | Macclesfield CP was extended to include part of Gawsworth CP, but this area remained in Macclesfield Rural sub-district. |
| 1959 October 1st | Extended to include the part of Macclesfield CP in Macclesfield Rural sub-district since 1955. |
| 1974 April 1st | Abolished. |

**Macclesfield Rural sub-district (1948–74):**
Registers now in MACCLESFIELD district.
1948 October 1st  Created from Adlington, Bosley, Chelford, Chorley, Eaton, Gawsworth, Great Warford, Henbury, Hurdsfield, Kettleshulme, Lyme Handley, Macclesfield Forest, Marton, Mottram St.Andrew, Nether Alderley, North Rode, Over Alderley, Pott Shrigley, Poynton with Worth, Prestbury, Rainow, Siddington, Snelson, Sutton, Wildboarclough, Wincle and Withington CPs (formerly in Macclesfield district).
1955 March 8th  Part of Gawsworth CP was added to Macclesfield CP, but this area remained in Macclesfield Rural sub-district.
1959 October 1st  The part of Macclesfield CP (which until 1955 was part of Gawsworth CP) was transferred to Macclesfield & Bollington sub-district).
1974 April 1st  Abolished.

**Prestbury sub-district (1837–1937):**
Registers now in MACCLESFIELD district.
1837 July 1st  Created from Adlington, Butley, Fallibroome, Mottram St. Andrew, Newton, Poynton, Prestbury, Upton, Woodford and Worth CPs.
1880 December 21st  Poynton CP and Worth CP were united to create Poynton with Worth CP.
1936 April 1st  The following changes to CPs took place, without alteration to the boundary of the sub-district:
*(a)* Part of Adlington CP was added to Bollington CP.
*(b)* Butley CP was abolished and incorporated into Bollington and Prestbury CPs.
*(c)* Fallibroome and Upton CPs were abolished and incorporated into Macclesfield and Prestbury CPs;.
*(d)* Newton CP was abolished and incorporated into Mottram St. Andrew CP.
1937 April 1st  Abolished (incorporated into Macclesfield sub-district).

**Rainow sub-district (1837–1928):**
Registers now in MACCLESFIELD district.
1837 July 1st  Created from Kettleshulme, Macclesfield Forest, Rainow, Taxal and Yeardsley cum Whaley CPs.
1928 April 1st  Abolished (Macclesfield Forest CP was transferred to Gawsworth sub-district, and the other CPs to Bollington sub-district).

**Sutton sub-district (1837–1910):**
Registers now in MACCLESFIELD district.
1837 July 1st          Created from Sutton, Wildboarclough and Wincle CPs.
1894 September 30th    Part of Sutton CP was added to Macclesfield CP, but remained in Sutton sub-district.
1907 April 1st         The part of Macclesfield CP (which had been part of Sutton CP until 1894) was transferred to Macclesfield sub-district.
1910 December 1st      Abolished (incorporated into Gawsworth sub-district).

**West Macclesfield sub-district (1837–1907):**
Registers now in MACCLESFIELD district.
1837 July 1st          Created from the part of Macclesfield CP on the west side of the Leek to Stockport turnpike road.
1907 April 1st         Abolished (incorporated into Macclesfield sub-district).


## MARKET DRAYTON DISTRICT

Created 1837 out of the CPs in Market Drayton Poor-Law Union (in *Ches.*, *Salop* and *Staffs.*). In *Salop* Registration County. In some early records the district was listed as DRAYTON.

**Moreton Say sub-district** (partly in *Ches.* 1837–95):
Registers now in NORTH SHROPSHIRE district.
1837 July 1st          Created, including Tittenley CP in *Ches.* (the remaining CPs were in *Salop* and *Staffs.*).
1895 September 30th    Tittenley CP was transferred to *Salop*.


## NANTWICH DISTRICT

Created 1837 out of the CPs in Nantwich Poor-Law Union. Abolished 1937 and incorporated into CREWE district.

**Bunbury sub-district (1837–1915):**
Registers now in SOUTH CHESHIRE district.
1837 July 1st          Created from Alpraham, Beeston, Bunbury, Burwardsley, Calveley, Church Minshull, Eaton, Haughton, Peckforton, Ridley, Rushton, Spurstow, Tarporley, Tilstone Fearnall, Tiverton, Utkinton, Wardle and Wettenhall CPs.
1892 July 1st          Beeston, Burwardsley, Eaton, Rushton, Tarporley, Tilstone Fearnall, Tiverton and Utkinton CPs were transferred to CHESTER district.

**Bunbury sub-district** *(continued)*
1897 May 1st	Extended to include Bickerton, Bulkeley, Cholmondeley and Egerton CPs (formerly in Wrenbury sub-district).
1909 January 1st	Church Minshull CP was transferred to Nantwich sub-district.
1915 March 1st	Abolished (incorporated into Wrenbury sub-district).

**Crewe sub-district (1882–1920):**
Registers now in SOUTH CHESHIRE district.
1882 July 1st	Created from Barthomley, Basford, Batherton, Blakenhall, Bridgemere, Checkley cum Wrinehill, Chorlton, Church Coppenhall, Crewe, Doddington, Haslington, Hatherton, Hough, Hunsterson, Lea, Monks Coppenhall, Rope, Shavington cum Gresty, Stapeley, Walgherton, Warmingham, Weston, Willaston, Wistaston, and Wybunbury CPs (formerly in Wybunbury sub-district).
1912 February 1st	Extended to include Leighton, Minshull Vernon and Woolstanwood CPs (formerly in Nantwich sub-district).
1920 July 1st	Abolished (incorporated into Crewe Borough, Haslington and Nantwich sub-districts).

**Crewe Borough sub-district (1920–37):**
Registers now in SOUTH CHESHIRE district.
1920 July 1st	Created from Monks Coppenhall CP (formerly in Crewe sub-district).
1936 April 1st	Monks Coppenhall CP was extended to include parts of neighbouring CPs, but these areas were not added to Crewe Borough sub-district.
1937 April 1st	Abolished (incorporated into CREWE district).

**Haslington sub-district (1920–37):**
Registers now in SOUTH CHESHIRE district.
1920 July 1st	Created from Barthomley, Basford, Church Coppenhall, Crewe, Haslington, Leighton, Minshull Vernon, Shavington cum Gresty, Warmingham, Weston, Wistaston and Woolstanwood CPs (formerly in Crewe sub-district).
1936 April 1st	*(a)* The whole of Church Coppenhall CP and parts of Crewe, Haslington, Leighton, Shavington cum Gresty, Warmingham, Wistaston and Woolstanwood CPs were added to Monks Coppenhall CP, but these areas remained in Haslington sub-district.
	*(b)* Haslington CP was extended to include part of Wheelock CP, but this area was not added to Haslington sub-district.
1937 April 1st	Abolished (incorporated into CREWE district).

**Nantwich sub-district (1837-1937):**
Registers now in SOUTH CHESHIRE district.

| | |
|---|---|
| 1837 July 1st | Created from Acton, Alvaston, Aston juxta Mondrum, Austerson, Baddington, Brindley, Burland, Cholmondeston, Coole Pilate, Edleston, Faddiley, Henhull, Hurleston, Leighton, Minshull Vernon, Nantwich, Poole, Stoke, Woolstanwood and Worleston CPs. |
| 1883 March 25th | Extended to include two small detached parts of Baddiley CP (from Wrenbury sub-district) which were added to Brindley and Faddiley CPs. |
| 1888 March 24th | (a) Extended to include a detached part of Wrenbury sub-district and Dodcott cum Wilkesley CP which was added to Acton CP.<br>(b) Extended to include a detached part of Wrenbury sub-district and Baddiley CP which was added to Brindley CP. |
| 1899 September 29th | Alvaston CP was abolished and incorporated into Worleston CP. |
| 1908 January 1st | (a) Extended to include Baddiley CP (formerly in Wrenbury sub-district).<br>(b) Coole Pilate CP was transferred to Wrenbury sub-district. |
| 1909 January 1st | Extended to include Church Minshull CP (formerly in Bunbury sub-district). |
| 1912 February 1st | Leighton, Minshull Vernon and Woolstanwood CPs were transferred to Crewe sub-district. |
| 1920 July 1st | Extended to include Batherton, Blakenhall, Bridgemere, Checkley cum Wrinehill, Chorlton, Dodding ton, Hatherton, Hough, Hunsterson, Lea, Rope, Stapeley, Walgherton, Willaston and Wybunbury CPs (formerly in Crewe sub-district). |
| 1937 April 1st | Abolished (incorporated into CREWE district). |

**Wrenbury sub-district (1837-1937):**
Registers now in SOUTH CHESHIRE district.

| | |
|---|---|
| 1837 July 1st | Created from Audlem, Baddiley, Bickerton, Bickley, Broomhall, Buerton, Bulkeley, Cholmondeley, Chorley, Dodcott cum Wilkesley, Egerton, Hampton, Hankelow, Larkton, Macefen, Marbury cum Quoisley, Newhall, Norbury, Sound, Tushingham cum Grindley, Wirswall, Woodcott and Wrenbury cum Frith CPs. |
| 1853 April 1st | Bickley, Hampton, Larkton, Macefen, Marbury cum Quoisley, Norbury, Tushingham cum Grindley and Wirswall CPs were transferred to WHITCHURCH district. |
| 1883 March 25th | Two detached parts of Baddiley CP were added to Brindley and Faddiley CPs, and transferred to Nantwich sub-district. |

**Wrenbury sub-district** *(continued)*

| | |
|---|---|
| 1888 March 24th | *(a)* A detached part of Dodcott cum Wilkesley CP was added to Acton CP and transferred to Nantwich sub-district. |
| | *(b)* A detached part of Baddiley CP was added to Brindley CP and transferred to Nantwich sub-district. |
| 1897 May 1st | Bickerton, Bulkeley, Cholmondeley and Egerton CPs were transferred to Bunbury sub-district. |
| 1908 January 1st | *(a)* Extended to include Coole Pilate CP (formerly in Nantwich sub-district) |
| | *(b)* Baddiley CP was transferred to Nantwich sub-district. |
| 1915 March 1st | Extended to include Alpraham, Bickerton, Bulkeley, Bunbury, Calveley, Cholmondeley, Haughton, Peckforton, Ridley, Spurstow, Wardle and Wettenhall CPs (formerly in Bunbury sub-district). |
| 1936 April 1st | Bunbury CP was extended to include part of Tilstone Fearnall CP, but this area was not added to Wrenbury sub-district. |
| 1937 April 1st | Abolished (incorporated into CREWE district). |

**Wybunbury sub-district (1837–82):**
Registers now in SOUTH CHESHIRE district.

| | |
|---|---|
| 1837 July 1st | Created from Barthomley, Basford, Batherton, Blakenhall, Bridgemere, Checkley cum Wrinehill, Chorlton, Church Coppenhall, Crewe, Doddington, Haslington, Hatherton, Hough, Hunsterson, Lea, Monks Coppenhall, Rope, Shavington cum Gresty, Stapeley, Walgherton, Warmingham, Weston, Willaston, Wistaston and Wybunbury CPs. |
| 1882 July 1st | Abolished (incorporated into Crewe sub-district). |

## NORTH EAST CHESHIRE DISTRICT
Created 1937 out of parts of STOCKPORT and HAYFIELD districts. Abolished 1974, and incorporated into STOCKPORT and MACCLESFIELD districts.

**Bredbury sub-district (1937–69):**
Registers now in STOCKPORT district.

| | |
|---|---|
| 1937 April 1st | Created from Bredbury & Romiley CP. |
| 1952 April 1st | Part of Bredbury & Romiley CP was added to Stockport CP and transferred to STOCKPORT district. |
| 1969 April 1st | Abolished (incorporated into Hazel Grove sub-district). |

### Cheadle sub-district (1937–74):
Registers now in STOCKPORT district.
| | |
|---|---|
| 1937 April 1st | Created from Cheadle & Gatley CP. |
| 1974 April 1st | Abolished (incorporated into STOCKPORT district). |

### Hazel Grove sub-district (1937–74):
Registers now in STOCKPORT district.
| | |
|---|---|
| 1937 April 1st | Created from Disley, Hazel Grove cum Bramhall and Marple CPs. |
| 1939 April 1st | Hazel Grove sub-district and Hazel Grove cum Bramhall CP were extended to include the whole of Woodford CP (formerly in MACCLESFIELD district). |
| 1969 April 1st | Extended to include Bredbury & Romiley CP (formerly in Bredbury sub-district). |
| 1974 April 1st | Abolished. Disley CP was transferred to MACCLESFIELD district, and the remaining CPs to STOCKPORT district (in Gtr. Man.). |

## NORTHWICH DISTRICT
Created 1837 out of the CPs in Northwich Poor-Law Union. Abolished 1974, and incorporated into VALE ROYAL and CONGLETON & CREWE districts.

### Middlewich sub-district (1837–1937):
Registers now in VALE ROYAL district.
| | |
|---|---|
| 1837 July 1st | Created from Bostock, Byley, Croxton, Davenham, Goostrey cum Barnshaw, Kinderton cum Hulme, Lach Dennis, Middlewich, Moorsbarrow with Parme, Newhall, Newton, Occlestone, Ravenscroft, Rudheath, Shipbrook, Sproston, Stanthorne, Stublach, Sutton and Whatcroft CPs. |
| 1867 July 1st | Goostrey cum Barnshaw CP was transferred to CONGLETON district. |
| 1883 March 25th | (a) Middlewich sub-district and Bostock CP were extended to include a detached part of Moulton CP (formerly in Over sub-district).<br>(b) Middlewich sub-district and Rudheath CP were extended to include Bradfield Farm, a detached part of Shurlach CP (formerly in Northwich sub-district). |
| 1889 March 25th | Two detached parts of Rudheath CP were added to Cranage and Twemlow CPs, and transferred to CONGLETON district. |

**Middlewich sub-district** *(continued)*

1892 March 25th
    *(a)* Middlewich sub-district and Rudheath CP were extended to include the whole of Shurlach cum Bradford CP (formerly in Northwich sub-district).
    *(b)* Middlewich sub-district and Lach Dennis CP were extended to include the whole of Birches and Hulse CPs (formerly in Northwich sub-district).
    *(c)* Newhall and Stublach CPs were abolished and added to Lach Dennis CP.
    *(d)* Croxton and Ravenscroft CPs were abolished and added to Byley CP.
    *(e)* Mooresbarrow with Parme CP was abolished and added to Sproston CP.
    *(f)* Sutton CP was abolished and added to Newton CP.
    *(g)* Occlestone CP was abolished and added to Wimboldsley CP, and transferred to Over sub-district.
    *(h)* Shipbrook CP was abolished and added to Whatcroft CP.

1894 September 30th
    *(a)* Kinderton CP was created from parts of Kinderton cum Hulme and Newton CPs.
    *(b)* The remaining parts of Kinderton cum Hulme and Newton CPs were added to Middlewich CP.

1936 April 1st
The following changes to CPs took place without any alteration to the boundaries of the sub-district:
    *(a)* Parts of Bostock CP were added to Moulton and Winsford CPs.
    *(b)* Bostock CP was extended to include part of Wharton CP.
    *(c)* Byley CP was extended to include part of Leese CP.
    *(d)* Davenham CP was extended to include parts of Eaton, Hartford, Leftwich and Over CPs.
    *(e)* Kinderton CP was abolished and incorporated into Bradwall, Byley, Middlewich, Sproston, Stanthorne, Tetton and Wimboldsley CPs.
    *(f)* Lach Dennis CP was extended to include parts of Cranage and Leese CPs.
    *(g)* Middlewich CP was extended to include part of Tetton CP.
    *(h)* Part of Lostock Gralam CP was added to Rudheath CP.
    *(i)* Part of Stanthorne CP was added to Winsford CP.

1937 April 1st
    Abolished (incorporated into Northwich and Winsford sub-districts).

**Northwich sub-district (1837-1974):**
Registers now in VALE ROYAL district.

| | |
|---|---|
| 1837 July 1st | Created from Allostock, Anderton, Birches, Castle Northwich, Cogshall, Comberbach, Hulse, Leftwich, Lostock Gralam, Marbury, Marston, Nether Peover, Northwich, Shurlach cum Bradford, Wincham, Winnington and Witton cum Twambrooks CPs. |
| 1892 March 25th | (a) Northwich sub-district and Winnington CP were extended to include the whole of Wallerscote CP (formerly in Weaverham sub-district). |
| | (b) Birches and Hulse CPs were abolished, and incorporated into Lach Dennis CP and Middlewich sub-district. |
| | (c) Shurlach cum Bradford CP was abolished and added to Rudheath CP and Middlewich sub-district. |
| 1894 September 29th | (a) Castle Northwich and Witton cum Twambrooks CPs were abolished and added to Northwich CP. |
| | (b) Part of Hartford CP was added to Northwich CP, but this area was not added to Northwich sub-district. |
| 1936 April 1st | The following changes to CPs took place without any alteration to the boundaries of the sub-district: |
| | (a) Cogshall CP was abolished and added to Comberbach CP. |
| | (b) Leftwich CP was abolished and incorporated into Northwich, Davenham and Hartford CPs. |
| | (c) Part of Lostock Gralam CP was added to Rudheath CP. |
| | (d) Northwich CP was extended to include parts of Barnton and Rudheath CPs. |
| | (e) Part of Wincham CP was added to Tabley Inferior CP. |
| | (f) Part of Pickmere CP was added to Wincham CP. |
| | (g) Winnington CP was abolished and incorporated into Hartford, Northwich and Weaverham CPs. |
| 1937 April 1st | (a) Extended to include the whole of Acton, Barnton, Crowton, Cuddington, Hartford, Lach Dennis, Little Leigh, Rudheath and Weaverham CPs (formerly in Weaverham and Middlewich sub-districts). |
| | (b) Extended to include the part of Wincham CP in BUCKLOW district (which until 1936 had been part of Pickmere CP). |
| | (c) The part of Tabley Inferior CP (which until 1936 had been part of Wincham CP) was transferred to BUCKLOW district. |
| | (d) The part of Davenham CP (which until 1936 had been part of Leftwich CP) was transferred to Winsford sub-district. |

**Northwich sub-district** *(continued)*

1955 April 1st      Northwich CP was extended to include parts of Davenham and Whatcroft CPs, but these areas were not added to Northwich sub-district.

1959 October 1st      The part of Northwich CP in Winsford sub-district was transferred to Northwich sub-district.

1967 February 23rd      Acton CP was renamed Acton Bridge CP.

1974 April 1st      Abolished. (incorporated into VALE ROYAL district).

**Over sub-district (1837–1937):**
Registers now in VALE ROYAL district.

1837 July 1st      Created from Clive, Darnhall, Eaton, Little Budworth, Marton, Moulton, Oulton Lowe, Over, Weaver, Wharton and Wimboldsley CPs.

1883 March 25th      A detached part of Moulton CP was added to Bostock CP, and transferred to Middlewich sub-district.

1892 March 25th      *(a)* Oulton Lowe CP was abolished and added to Little Budworth CP.

*(b)* Weaver CP was abolished and added to Darnhall CP.

*(c)* Over sub-district and Wimboldsley CP were extended to include the whole of Occlestone CP (formerly in Middlewich sub-district).

1936 April 1st      The following changes to CPs took place without any alterations to the boundaries of the sub-district:

*(a)* Winsford CP was created from parts of Bostock, Clive, Darnhall, Eaton, Marton, Moulton, Over, Stanthorne and Wharton CPs.

*(b)* The remainder of Clive CP was added to Stanthorne CP.

*(c)* The remainder of Eaton CP was incorporated into Davenham and Hartford CPs.

*(d)* The remainder of Wharton CP and part of Moulton CP were added to Bostock CP.

*(e)* Parts of Little Budworth CP were added to Delamere, Oakmere and Rushton CPs.

*(f)* Part of Marton CP was added to Oakmere CP.

*(g)* Part of Over CP was added to Davenham CP.

*(h)* Wimboldsley CP was extended to include part of Kinderton CP.

1937 April 1st      Abolished (incorporated into Winsford sub-district).

**Weaverham sub-district (1837–1937):**
Registers now in VALE ROYAL district.

| | |
|---|---|
| 1837 July 1st | Created from Acton, Barnton, Crowton, Cuddington, Delamere, Eddisbury, Hartford, Little Leigh, Oakmere, Onston, Wallerscote and Weaverham cum Milton CPs. |
| 1881 December 21st | Crowton CP and Weaverham sub-district were extended to include a detached part of Norley CP (formerly in RUNCORN district). |
| 1892 March 25th | *(a)* Onston CP was abolished and added to Crowton CP.<br>*(b)* Winnington CP and Northwich sub-district were extended to include the whole of Wallerscote CP (formerly in Weaverham sub-district). |
| 1894 September 29th | Part of Hartford CP was added to Northwich CP, but remained in Weaverham sub-district. |
| 1936 April 1st | The following changes to CPs took place without any alteration to the boundaries of the sub-district:<br>*(a)* Part of Acton CP was added to Dutton CP.<br>*(b)* Part of Barnton CP was added to Northwich CP.<br>*(c)* Part of Delamere CP was added to Utkinton CP.<br>*(d)* Delamere CP was extended to include the whole of Eddisbury CP and parts of Little Budworth and Utkinton CPs.<br>*(e)* Oakmere CP was extended to include parts of Little Budworth and Marton CPs.<br>*(f)* Weaverham CP was created from parts of Barnton, Weaverham cum Milton and Winnington CPs.<br>*(g)* The remainder of Weaverham cum Milton CP was incorporated into Acton, Barnton, Cuddington and Hartford CPs. |
| 1937 April 1st | Abolished (Delamere and Oakmere CPs were transferred to Winsford sub-district, and the remaining CPs to Northwich sub-district). |

**Winsford sub-district (1937–74):**
Registers now in VALE ROYAL district.

| | |
|---|---|
| 1937 April 1st | Created from Bostock, Byley, Darnhall, Davenham, Delamere, Little Budworth, Marton, Middlewich, Moulton, Oakmere, Rushton, Sproston, Stanthorne, Tarporley, Utkinton, Whatcroft, Wimboldsley and Winsford CPs. |
| 1974 April 1st | Abolished (Middlewich CP was transferred to CONGLETON & CREWE district, and the remaining CPs to VALE ROYAL district). |

# RUNCORN DISTRICT

Created 1837 out of the CPs in Runcorn Poor-Law Union. Abolished 1974, and incorporated into HALTON and VALE ROYAL districts.

## Budworth sub-district (1837-1937):
Registers now in WARRINGTON district.

| | |
|---|---|
| 1837 July 1st | Created from Antrobus, Appleton, Bartington, Crowley, Great Budworth, Higher Whitley, Lower Whitley, Seven Oaks and Stretton CPs. |
| 1891 August 1st | Extended to include Acton Grange, Daresbury, Dutton, Hatton, Keckwick, Moore, Newton by Daresbury, Preston on the Hill, Walton Inferior and Walton Superior CPs (formerly in Daresbury sub-district). |
| 1896 November 1st | Extended to include Grappenhall, Latchford, Latchford Without and Thelwall CPs (formerly in WARRINGTON district). |
| 1896 November 9th | Latchford CP was extended to include parts of Appleton, Latchford Without and Walton Inferior CPs, and transferred to *Lancs*. (but remained in Budworth sub-district). |
| 1896 December 1st | Latchford CP [*Lancs.*] was transferred to WARRINGTON district. |
| 1897 October 1st | Stockton Heath CP was created from part of Appleton CP. |
| 1933 April 1st | The following changes to CPs took place without any alterations to boundaries of the sub-district:<br>(a) Parts of Acton Grange, Moore and Walton Inferior CPs were added to Penketh CP [*Lancs.*].<br>(b) Parts of Grappenhall CP were added to Warrington and Woolston CPs [*Lancs.*].<br>(c) Part of Woolston with Martinscroft CP [*Lancs.*] was added to Grappenhall CP.<br>(d) Parts of Latchford Without and Stockton Heath CPs were added to Warrington CP [*Lancs.*]. |
| 1936 April 1st | The following changes to CPs took place without any alterations to boundaries of the sub-district:<br>(a) Acton Grange, Walton Inferior and Walton Superior CPs were united to create Walton CP.<br>(b) Crowley and Seven Oaks CPs were abolished and added to Antrobus CP.<br>(c) Dutton CP was extended to include the whole of Bartington CP and part of Acton CP.<br>(d) Keckwick and Newton by Daresbury CPs were abolished and added to Daresbury CP.<br>(e) Part of Lymm CP and the whole of Thelwall CP were added to Grappenhall CP. |

**Budworth sub-district** *(continued)*
1936 April 1st  *(f)* Higher Whitley and Lower Whitley CPs were united to create Whitley CP.
*(g)* The whole of Latchford Without CP was added to Stockton Heath CP.
*(h)* The whole of Preston on the Hill CP was added to Preston Brook CP.
1937 April 1st  Abolished (incorporated into Runcorn and Stockton Heath sub-districts).

**Daresbury sub-district (1837–91):**
Registers now in HALTON district.
1845 October 6th  Created from Acton Grange, Daresbury, Dutton, Hatton, Keckwick, Moore, Newton by Daresbury, Preston on the Hill, Walton Inferior and Walton Superior CPs (formerly in Grappenhall sub-district).
1891 August 1st  Abolished (incorporated into Budworth sub-district).

**Frodsham sub-district (1837–1937):**
Registers now in HALTON district.
1837 July 1st  Created from Alvanley, Frodsham, Frodsham Lordship, Helsby, Kingsley, Kingswood, Manley, Newton by Frodsham and Norley CPs.
1881 December 20th  A detached part of Norley CP was added to Crowton CP and transferred to NORTHWICH district.
1936 April 1st  *(a)* Frodsham Lordship CP was abolished and added to Frodsham CP.
*(b)* Kingswood CP was abolished and incorporated into Kingsley, Manley and Norley CPs.
*(c)* Newton by Frodsham CP was abolished and added to Kingsley CP.
1937 April 1st  Abolished (incorporated into Runcorn sub-district).

**Grappenhall sub-district (1837–45):**
Registers now in HALTON district.
1837 July 1st  Created from Acton Grange, Daresbury, Dutton, Grappenhall, Hatton, Keckwick, Latchford, Moore, Newton by Daresbury, Preston on the Hill, Thelwall, Walton Inferior and Walton Superior CPs.
1845 October 6th  Abolished (Grappenhall, Latchford and Thelwall CPs were transferred to WARRINGTON district, and the remaining CPs to Daresbury sub-district).

**Runcorn sub-district (1837-1974):**
Registers now in WARRINGTON district.

| | |
|---|---|
| 1837 July 1st | Created from Aston by Sutton, Aston Grange, Clifton, Halton, Norton, Runcorn, Stockham, Sutton and Weston CPs. |
| 1933 April 1st | Part of Norton CP was added to Cuerdley CP [*Lancs.*], but remained in Runcorn sub-district. |
| 1936 April 1st | *(a)* Aston by Sutton and Aston Grange CPs were united to create Aston CP. |
| | *(b)* Clifton CP was abolished and incorporated into Runcorn and Sutton CPs. |
| | *(c)* Part of Norton CP was added to Preston Brook CP. |
| | *(d)* Stockham CP was abolished and added to Norton CP. |
| | *(e)* Weston CP was abolished and added to Runcorn CP. |
| 1937 April 1st | *(a)* Extended to include the whole of Alvanley, Frodsham, Helsby, Kingsley, Manley and Norley CPs (formerly in Frodsham sub-district). |
| | *(b)* The part of Cuerdley CP [*Lancs.*] (which until 1933 had been part of Norton CP) was transferred to WARRINGTON district. |
| | *(c)* The part of Preston Brook CP (which until 1936 was part of Norton CP) was transferred to Stockton Heath sub-district. |
| 1967 April 1st | *(a)* Halton CP was abolished and added to Runcorn CP. |
| | *(b)* Runcorn sub-district and Runcorn CP were extended to include parts of Daresbury, Dutton, Moore and Preston Brook CPs (formerly in Stockton Heath sub-district). |
| | *(c)* The remainder of Norton CP was added to Daresbury CP and transferred to Stockton Heath sub-district. |
| 1974 April 1st | Abolished (incorporated into HALTON district). |

**Stockton Heath sub-district (1937-74):**
Registers now in WARRINGTON district.

| | |
|---|---|
| 1937 April 1st | Created from Antrobus, Appleton, Daresbury, Dutton, Grappenhall, Great Budworth, Hatton, Moore, Preston Brook, Stockton Heath, Stretton, Walton and Whitley CPs. |
| 1967 April 1st | *(a)* Parts of Daresbury, Dutton, Moore and Preston Brook CPs were added to Runcorn CP and transferred to Runcorn sub-district. |
| | *(b)* Daresbury CP and Stockton Heath sub-district were extended to include part of Norton CP (formerly in Runcorn sub-district). |
| 1974 April 1st | Abolished (incorporated into HALTON district). |

# STOCKPORT DISTRICT

Created 1837 out of the CPs in Stockport Poor-Law Union (in *Ches.* and *Lancs.*). From 1937 to 1974 the district comprised the area in Stockport County Borough. Transferred to *Gtr. Man.* in 1974.

## Bredbury sub-district (1837-1937):
Registers now in STOCKPORT district.

| | |
|---|---|
| 1905 June 1st | Created from Bredbury, Compstall and Romiley CPs (formerly in Hyde and Marple sub-districts). |
| 1936 April 1st | The following changes to CPs took place without any alterations to the boundaries of the sub-district:<br>*(a)* Bredbury CP was abolished and incorporated into Bredbury & Romiley, Marple and Stockport CPs.<br>*(b)* Compstall CP was abolished and incorporated into Bredbury & Romiley and Hyde CPs.<br>*(c)* Romiley CP was abolished and incorporated into Bredbury & Romiley and Marple CPs. |
| 1937 April 1st | Abolished (incorporated into NORTH EAST CHESHIRE and HYDE districts). |

## Cheadle sub-district (1837-1937):
Registers now in STOCKPORT district.

| | |
|---|---|
| 1837 July 1st | Created from Stockport Etchells CP, part of Handforth cum Bosden CP (i.e. Handforth), and the parts of Cheadle Bulkeley and Cheadle Moseley CPs outside the borough of Stockport. |
| 1877 December 17th | Handforth cum Bosden CP was abolished, and divided into Handforth CP (in Cheadle sub-district) and Bosden CP (in Hazel Grove sub-district). |
| 1879 May 3rd | Cheadle Bulkeley and Cheadle Moseley CPs were united to create Cheadle CP. The boundary of Cheadle sub-district was unchanged. |
| 1894 October 29th | Part of Cheadle CP was added to Stockport CP, but remained in Cheadle sub-district. |
| 1901 November 9th | A further part of Cheadle CP was added to Stockport CP, but remained in Cheadle sub-district. |
| 1903 January 1st | The parts of Stockport CP in Cheadle sub-district (i.e. Brinksway, Cheadle Heath and part of Adswood) were transferred to Stockport First sub-district. |
| 1930 March 31st | Cheadle CP and Stockport Etchells CPs were united to create Cheadle & Gatley CP. |

**Cheadle sub-district** *(continued)*

1936 April 1st  The following changes to CPs took place without any alterations to boundaries of the sub-district:
*(a)* Part of Cheadle & Gatley CP was added to Wilmslow CP.
*(b)* Handforth CP was abolished and incorporated into Cheadle & Gatley and Wilmslow CPs.

1937 April 1st  Abolished (incorporated mainly into NORTH EAST CHESHIRE district).

**Hazel Grove sub-district (1837–1937):**
Registers now in STOCKPORT district.

1837 July 1st  Created from Bramhall, Norbury and Torkington CPs, and the hamlet of Bosden in Handforth cum Bosden CP.

1877 December 17th  Handforth cum Bosden CP was abolished, and divided into Handforth CP (in Cheadle sub-district) and Bosden CP (in Hazel Grove sub-district).

1900 September 30th  Bosden, Bramhall, Norbury and Torkington CPs were abolished and incorporated into Hazel Grove cum Bramhall CP.

1901 November 9th  Part of Hazel Grove cum Bramhall CP was added to Stockport CP, but remained in Hazel Grove sub-district.

1903 January 1st  The parts of Stockport CP in Hazel Grove sub-district (i.e. Davenport and Woods Moor) were transferred to Stockport First sub-district.

1905 June 1st  Extended to include Marple CP and the remaining part of Hazel Grove cum Bramhall CP (formerly in Marple sub-district).

1923 October 1st  Marple CP was transferred to Marple sub-district.

1935 April 1st  Part of Hazel Grove cum Bramhall CP was added to Stockport CP, but remained in Hazel Grove sub-district.

1936 April 1st  Part of Hazel Grove cum Bramhall CP was added to Marple CP, but remained in Hazel Grove sub-district.

1937 April 1st  Abolished (incorporated into NORTH EAST CHESHIRE district).

**Heaton Norris sub-district (1837–1937)** [wholly in *Lancs.* 1837–1913].
Registers now in STOCKPORT district.

1837 July 1st  Created from Heaton Norris and Reddish CPs [both in *Lancs.*].

1894 October 20th  Part of Heaton Norris CP [*Lancs.*] was added to Stockport CP [*Ches.*], but remained in Heaton Norris sub-district.

1901 November 9th  Reddish CP was transferred from *Lancs.* to *Ches.*

1903 January 1st  Reddish CP and the part of Stockport CP in Heaton Norris sub-district were transferred to Stockport Third sub-district.

1913 November 9th  *(a)* Part of Heaton Norris CP was added to Manchester CP [*Lancs.*] and transferred to CHORLTON district.

**Heaton Norris sub-district** *(continued)*

| | |
|---|---|
| 1913 November 9th | *(b)* The remaining part of Heaton Norris CP was transferred from *Lancs.* to *Ches.* |
| 1936 April 1st | Heaton Norris and Reddish CPs were abolished and incorporated into Stockport CP, but remained in Heaton Norris sub-distict. |
| 1937 April 1st | Abolished (incorporated into Stockport First and Stockport Second sub-districts). |

**Hyde sub-district (1837–1937):**
Registers now in TAMESIDE district.

| | |
|---|---|
| 1837 July 1st | Created from Bredbury, Hyde and Werneth CPs. |
| 1897 September 30th | Werneth CP was renamed Compstall CP. |
| 1901 November 9th | Part of Bredbury CP was added to Stockport CP, but remained in Hyde sub-district. |
| 1902 September 30th | Bredbury CP was extended to include the whole of Brinnington CP, but this area remained in Stockport Second sub-district. |
| 1903 January 1st | *(a)* Extended to include the part of Bredbury CP in Stockport Second sub-district (which until 1902 had been part of Brinnington CP). |
| | *(b)* The part of Stockport CP (i.e. Woodbank Park, which until 1901 had been part of Bredbury CP) was transferred to Stockport Second sub-district. |
| 1905 June 1st | Bredbury and Compstall CPs were transferred to Bredbury sub-district; thus Hyde sub-district was now co-extensive with Hyde CP. |
| 1923 October 1st | Hyde CP was extended to include the whole of Godley and Newton CPs, but these areas were not added to Hyde sub-district. |
| 1936 April 1st | *(a)* Parts of Hyde CP were added to Bredbury & Romiley CP and Dukinfield CP, but remained in Hyde sub- district. |
| | *(b)* Hyde CP was extended to include parts of Compstall, Dukinfield, Hattersley and Matley CPs, but these areas were not added to Hyde sub-district. |
| 1937 April 1st | Abolished (incorporated into HYDE district). |

**Marple sub-district (1837–1905):**
Registers now in STOCKPORT district.

| | |
|---|---|
| 1837 July 1st | Created from Marple, Offerton and Romiley CPs. |
| 1900 September 30th | Offerton CP became part of Hazel Grove cum Bramhall CP, but remained in Marple sub-district. |
| 1905 June 1st | Abolished (Romiley CP was transferred to Bredbury sub-district, and the remaining areas to Hazel Grove sub-district). |

**Marple sub-district (1923–37):**
Registers now in STOCKPORT district.
| | |
|---|---|
| 1923 October 1st | Created from Marple CP (formerly in Hazel Grove sub-district). |
| 1935 April 1st | Marple CP was extended to include the whole of Ludworth and Mellor CPs [both in *Derb.*], but these areas were not added to Marple sub-district. |
| 1936 April 1st | Marple CP was extended to include parts of Bredbury, Hazel Grove cum Bramhall, Romiley and Stockport CPs, but these areas were not added to Marple sub-district. |
| 1937 April 1st | Abolished (incorporated into NORTH EAST CHESHIRE district). |

**Newton sub-district (1923–37):**
Registers now in TAMESIDE district.
| | |
|---|---|
| 1923 October 1st | Created from the part of Hyde CP which until 1923 comprised Godley and Newton CPs (formerly in ASHTON UNDER LYNE district). |
| 1937 April 1st | Abolished (incorporated into HYDE district). |

**Stockport First sub-district (1837–1974):**
Registers now in STOCKPORT district.
| | |
|---|---|
| 1837 July 1st | Created from parts of Cheadle Bulkeley, Cheadle Moseley and Stockport CPs (i.e. the Edgeley, Middle and St. Thomas wards of Stockport Borough). |
| 1879 May 3rd | The parts of Cheadle Bulkeley and Cheadle Moseley CPs in Stockport First sub-district became part of Cheadle CP. |
| 1894 October 29th | The part of Cheadle CP in Stockport First sub-district was added to Stockport CP. |
| 1903 January 1st | Altered so as to comprises the part of Stockport CP in the Cale Green, Edgeley, Heaviley, Hempshaw Lane, Hollywood, St. Thomas and Shaw Heath wards of Stockport County Borough. |
| 1912 April 1st | The Edgeley and Hollywood wards of Stockport County Borough were transferred to Stockport Second sub-district. |
| 1937 April 1st | Altered so as to comprise the part of Stockport CP in the Cale Green, Davenport, Edgeley, Hempshaw Lane, Hollywood, St. Mary's, St. Thomas', Shaw Heath and Vernon wards of Stockport County Borough. |
| 1974 April 1st | Abolished (transferred to *Gtr. Man.*). |

## Stockport Second sub-district (1837-1974):
Registers now in STOCKPORT district.
| | |
|---|---|
| 1837 July 1st | Created from Brinnington CP and part of Stockport CP (i.e. the Portwood and St. Mary wards of Stockport Borough). |
| 1902 September 30th | Brinnington CP was abolished and incorporated into Bredbury CP, but the area remained in Stockport Second sub-district. |
| 1903 January 1st | Altered so as to comprise the part of Stockport CP in the Heaton Lane, Portwood, St. Mary, Spring Bank and Vernon wards of Stockport County Borough. |
| 1912 April 1st | (a) Extended to include the Edgeley and Hollywood wards of Stockport County Borough (formerly in Stockport First sub-district). <br> (b) Heaton Lane ward was transferred to Stockport Third sub-district. |
| 1937 April 1st | Altered so as to comprise the part of Stockport CP in the Heaton Lane, Heaton Norris North, Heaton Norris South and Old Road wards of Stockport County Borough. |
| 1974 April 1st | Abolished (transferred to *Gtr. Man.*). |

## Stockport Third sub-district (1903-74):
Registers now in STOCKPORT district.
| | |
|---|---|
| 1903 January 1st | Created from Reddish CP and the part of Stockport CP in the Lancashire Hill and Old Road wards of Stockport County Borough. |
| 1912 April 1st | Extended to include the part of Stockport CP in the Heaton Lane ward of Stockport County Borough (formerly in Stockport Second sub-district). |
| 1936 April 1st | Reddish CP was abolished and added to Stockport CP, but the area remained in Stockport Third sub-district |
| 1937 April 1st | Altered so as to comprise the part of Stockport CP in the Heaviley, Lancashire Hill, Portwood, Reddish North and Reddish South wards of Stockport County Borough. |
| 1952 April 1st | Stockport CP and Stockport Third sub-district were extended to include part of Bredbury & Romiley CP (formerly in NORTH EAST CHESHIRE district). |
| 1974 April 1st | Abolished (transferred to *Gtr. Man.*). |

## WALLASEY DISTRICT
Created 1937 out of BIRKENHEAD and WIRRAL districts, comprising the area in Wallasey County Borough.

**Wallasey sub-district (1937-74):**
Registers now in WALLASEY district.
1937 April 1st        Created from Wallasey CP.
1974 April 1st        Wallasey CP was transferred to Mers.


## WARRINGTON DISTRICT
In *Lancs*. Registration County. Partly in *Ches*. 1845-96.

**Latchford sub-district (1845-96):**
Registers now in WARRINGTON district.
1845 October 6th    Created from Grappenhall, Latchford and Thelwall CPs (formerly in RUNCORN district).
1884 March 24th    Latchford sub-district and Latchford CP were extended to include part of Warrington CP [*Lancs.*] (formerly in Warrington sub-district)
1884 March 25th    Part of Thelwall CP was added to Woolston with Martinscroft CP [*Lancs.*] and transferred to Rixton sub-district.
1894 November 21st  Latchford Without CP was created from part of Latchford CP.
1896 November 1st   Abolished (incorporated into RUNCORN district).


## WEST CHESHIRE DISTRICT
Created 1937 out of CHESTER and WHITCHURCH districts. Abolished 1974 and incorporated into CHESTER & ELLESMERE PORT district.

**Chester Castle sub-district (1937-74):**
Registers now in CHESTER & ELLESMERE PORT district.
1937 April 1st        Created from Aldford, Bache, Backford, Barrow, Bridge Trafford, Buerton, Capenhurst, Caughall, Chester Castle, Childer Thornton, Chorlton by Backford, Christleton, Churton Heath, Claverton, Croughton, Dodleston, Dunham on the Hill, Eaton, Eccleston, Ellesmere Port, Elton, Great Boughton, Great Saughall, Great Stanney, Great Sutton, Guilden Sutton, Hapsford, Hoole, Hoole Village, Hooton, Huntington, Ince, Lea by Backford, Lea Newbold, Ledsham, Little Saughall, Little Stanney, Little Sutton, Littleton,

**Chester Castle sub-district** (continued)

| | |
|---|---|
| 1937 April 1st | Lower Kinnerton, Marlston cum Lache, Mickle Trafford, Mollington, Moston, Picton, Poulton, Puddington, Pulford, Rowton, Saighton, Shotwick, Shotwick Park, Stoke, Tarvin, Thornton le Moors, Upton by Chester, Wervin, Wimbolds Trafford and Woodbank CPs |
| 1948 April 1st | Great Saughall and Little Saughall CPs were united to create Saughall CP. |
| 1950 April 1st | Ellesmere Port CP was extended to include the whole of Childer Thornton, Great Stanney, Great Sutton, Hooton, Ince and Little Sutton CPs. |
| 1954 April 1st | *(a)* Parts of Hoole and Upton by Chester CPs were added to Chester CP and transferred to CHESTER district.<br>*(b)* The remainder of Hoole CP was incorporated into Guilden Sutton and Hoole Village CPs. |
| 1974 April 1st | Abolished; all CPs were transferred to CHESTER & ELLESMERE PORT district. |

**Tarvin Rural sub-district (1937–74):**

Registers now in CHESTER & ELLESMERE PORT district.

| | |
|---|---|
| 1937 April 1st | Created from Agden, Aldersey, Ashton, Barton, Beeston, Bickley, Bradley, Broxton, Bruen Stapleford, Burton by Tarvin, Burwardsley, Caldecott, Carden, Chidlow, Chorlton, Chowley, Church Shocklach, Churton by Aldford, Churton by Farndon, Clotton Hoofield, Clutton, Coddington, Cotton Abbotts, Cotton Edmunds, Crewe by Farndon, Cuddington, Duckington, Duddon, Edge, Edgerley, Farndon, Foulk Stapleford, Golborne Bellow, Golborne David, Grafton, Hampton, Handley, Harthill, Hatton, Hockenhull, Horton, Horton cum Peel, Huxley, Iddinshall, Kelsall, King's Marsh, Larkton, Macefen, Malpas, Mouldsworth, Newton by Malpas, Newton by Tattenhall, Oldcastle, Overton, Prior's Heys, Shocklach Oviatt, Stockton, Stretton, Tarvin, Tattenhall, Threapwood, Tilston, Tilstone Fearnall, Tiverton, Tushingham cum Grindley, Waverton, Wigland, Willington and Wychough CPs. |
| 1974 April 1st | Abolished (incorporated into CHESTER & ELLESMERE PORT district). |

## WHITCHURCH DISTRICT
Created 1853 out GREAT BOUGHTON, NANTWICH and WREXHAM districts. In *Salop* Registration County. 1937 the CPs in *Ches.* were transferred to CREWE and WEST CHESHIRE districts.

**Malpas sub-district (1857–1937):**
Registers now in CHESTER & ELLESMERE PORT district.
1857 November 1st    Created from Agden, Bickley, Bradley, Chidlow, Chorlton, Cuddington, Duckington, Edge, Hampton, Larkton, Macefen, Malpas, Newton by Malpas, Oldcastle, Overton, Stockton, Tushingham cum Grindley, Wigland and Wychough CPs (formerly in Whitchurch sub-district).
1897 January 1st    Extended to include Threapwood CP (formerly in WREXHAM district).
1937 April 1st    Abolished (incorporated into WEST CHESHIRE district).

**Whitchurch sub-district** (partly in *Ches.* 1857–1937):
Registers now in CHESTER & ELLESMERE PORT district.
1853 April 1st    Created; including Agden, Bickley, Bradley, Chidlow, Chorlton, Cuddington, Duckington, Edge, Hampton, Larkton, Macefen, Malpas, Marbury cum Quoisley, Newton by Malpas, Norbury, Oldcastle, Overton, Stockton, Tushingham cum Grindley, Wigland, Wirswall and Wychough CPs (all the remaining CPs were in *Salop* and *Flint*].
1857 November 1st    All CPs in *Ches.* except Marbury cum Quoisley, Norbury and Wirswall were transferred to Malpas sub-district.
1937 April 1st    Abolished (the CPs in *Ches* were transferred to CREWE district).

## WIRRAL DISTRICT
Created 1837 out of the CPs in Wirral Poor-Law Union. Abolished 1974 and incorporated into BIRKENHEAD district [*Mers.*].

**Bebington sub-district (1892–1937):**
Registers now in BIRKENHEAD district.
1892 December 1st    Created from Brimstage, Bromborough, Higher Bebington, Lower Bebington, Poulton cum Spital and Storeton CPs (formerly in Eastham sub-district).
1894 September (?)    Rock Ferry CP was created from part of Higher Bebington CP.
1898 March 31st    The whole of Rock Ferry CP and part of Lower Bebington CP were added to Birkenhead CP, and transferred to BIRKENHEAD district.

**Bebington sub-district** *(continued)*
1922 April 1st        Higher Bebington, Lower Bebington and Bromborough CPs were united to create Bebington cum Bromborough CP.
1933 April 1st        Part of Brimstage CP was added to Barnston CP, but remained in Bebington sub-district.
1937 April 1st        Abolished (incorporated into East Wirral and West Wirral sub-districts).

**Birkenhead sub-district (1837–61):**
Registers now in BIRKENHEAD district.
1837 July 1st         Created from Birkenhead and Tranmere CPs.
1861 August 1st       Abolished (incorporated into BIRKENHEAD district).

**Clatterbridge sub-district (1959–74):**
Registers now in BIRKENHEAD district.
1959 April 1st        Created from the Clatterbridge Hospital premises in Poulton cum Spital CP (formerly in East Wirral district).
1974 April 1st        Abolished (incorporated into BIRKENHEAD district).

**Eastham sub-district (1837–1937):**
Registers now in CHESTER & ELLESMERE PORT district.
1837 July 1st         Created from Brimstage, Bromborough, Childer Thornton, Eastham, Great Sutton, Higher Bebington, Hooton, Little Sutton, Lower Bebington, Netherpool, Overpool, Poulton cum Spital, Storeton and Whitby CPs.
1892 December 1st     Brimstage, Bromborough, Higher Bebington, Lower Bebington, Poulton cum Spital and Storeton CPs were transferred to Bebington sub-district.
1900 February 1st     Extended to include Ledsham CP (formerly in Neston sub-district)
1911 April 1st        Netherpool, Overpool and Whitby CPs were united to create Ellesmere Port CP.
1933 April 1st        *(a)* Extended to include Puddington CP (formerly in Neston sub-district).
                      *(b)* Parts of Willaston CP were added to Childer Thornton and Ledsham CPs, but these areas remained in Neston sub-district.
                      *(c)* Part of Eastham CP was added to Willaston CP, but remained in Eastham sub-district.
                      *(d)* Part of Little Sutton CP was added to Ledsham CP, but remained in Eastham sub-district.
1937 April 1st        Abolished

**East Wirral sub-district (1937–74):**
Registers now in BIRKENHEAD district.
| | |
|---|---|
| 1937 April 1st | Created from Bebington cum Bromborough, Brimstage, Eastham, Poulton cum Spital, Raby, Storeton and Thornton Hough CPs. |
| 1959 April 1st | The Clatterbridge Hospital premises in Poulton cum Spital CP were transferred to Clatterbridge sub-district. |
| 1974 April 1st | Abolished (incorporated into BIRKENHEAD district). |

**Neston sub-district (1837–1937):**
Registers now in BIRKENHEAD district.
| | |
|---|---|
| 1837 July 1st | Created from Burton, Gayton, Great Neston, Heswall cum Oldfield, Ledsham, Leighton, Little Neston, Ness, Puddington, Raby, Thornton Hough and Willaston CPs. |
| 1894 September 30th | Great Neston, Leighton and Little Neston CPs were united to create Neston cum Parkgate CP. |
| 1900 February 1st | Ledsham CP was transferred to Eastham sub-district. |
| 1933 April 1st | (a) Burton CP was extended to include part of Puddington CP. |
| | (b) Part of Willaston CP was added to Puddington CP. |
| | (c) Puddington CP as altered was transferred to Eastham sub-district. |
| | (d) Ledsham CP was extended to include part of Little Sutton CP, but this area remained in Eastham sub-district. |
| | (e) Other parts of Willaston CP were transferred to Childer Thornton and Little Sutton CPs, but remained in Neston sub-district. |
| 1937 April 1st | Abolished; the CPs were transferred to East Wirral and West Wirral sub-districts. |

**Wallasey sub-district (1837–61):**
Registers now in WALLASEY district.
| | |
|---|---|
| 1837 July 1st | Created from Bidston cum Ford, Claughton cum Grange, Liscard, Poulton cum Seacombe and Wallasey CP. |
| 1861 August 1st | Abolished (incorporated into BIRKENHEAD district). |

**West Wirral sub-district (1937–74):**
Registers now in BIRKENHEAD district.
| | |
|---|---|
| 1937 April 1st | Created from Barnston, Burton, Caldy, Frankby, Gayton, Grange, Greasby, Heswall cum Oldfield, Hoylake cum West Kirby, Irby, Ness, Neston cum Parkgate, Pensby, Thurstaston and Willaston CPs. |
| 1974 April 1st | Abolished (incorporated into BIRKENHEAD district) |

**Woodchurch sub-district (1837–1937):**
Registers now in BIRKENHEAD district.
1837 July 1st    Created from Arrowe, Barnston, Caldy, Frankby, Grange, Greasby, Great Meols, Hoose, Irby, Landican, Little Meols, Moreton, Newton cum Larton, Noctorum, Oxton, Pensby, Prenton, Saughall Massie, Thingwall, Thurstaston, Upton by Birkenhead, West Kirby and Woodchurch CPs.
1861 August 1st    Noctorum and Oxton CPs were transferred to BIRKENHEAD district.
1889 March 24th    The whole of Newton cum Larton CP was added to Grange CP.
1894 September 30th    Hoylake cum West Kirby CP was created from the whole of Great Meols, Hoose, Little Meols, West Kirby and part of Grange CP.
1928 April 1st    The whole of Moreton CP was added to Wallasey CP and transferred to BIRKENHEAD district.
1933 April 1st    *(a)* Arrowe CP was abolished and incorporated into Birkenhead and Irby CPs, but the area remained wholly in Woodchurch sub-district.
*(b)* Barnston CP was extended to include part of Brimstage CP, but this area was not added to Woodchurch sub-district.
*(c)* Landican, Prenton, Thingwall and Woodchurch CPs were abolished and incorporated into Birkenhead CP, but these areas remained in Woodchurch sub-district.
*(d)* Part of Saughall Massie CP was added to Grange CP.
*(e)* The remainder of Saughall Massie CP and part of Upton by Birkenhead CP were added to Wallasey CP and transferred to WALLASEY sub-district.
*(f)* The remainder of Upton by Birkenhead CP was added to Birkenhead CP, but remained in Woodchurch sub-district.
1937 April 1st    Abolished (incorporated into East Wirral and West Wirral sub-districts).


**WREXHAM DISTRICT**
Created 1837 out of the CPs in Wrexham Poor-Law Union (in *Ches.*, *Denb.* and *Flint*). In *Denb.* Registration County. By 1897 all the CPs in *Ches.* had been transferred to WHITCHURCH and CHESTER districts.

**Holt sub-district** (partly in *Ches.* 1853–96):
Registers now in WREXHAM MAELOR district.
1853 April 1st    Created, including Church Shocklach, Shocklach Oviatt and Threapwood CPs in *Ches.* (formerly in Malpas sub-district).

**Holt sub-district** *(continued)*
1897 January 1st  (a) Church Shocklach and Shocklach Oviatt CPs were transferred to CHESTER district.
(b) Threapwood CP was transferred to WHITCHURCH district.

**Malpas sub-district (1837–53):**
Registers now in WREXHAM MAELOR district.
1837 July 1st   Created from Agden, Bradley, Chidlow, Chorlton, Church Shocklach, Cuddington, Malpas, Newton by Malpas, Oldcastle, Overton, Shocklach Oviatt, Stockton, Threapwood, Wigland and Wychough CPs.
1853 April 1st  Abolished (Church Shocklach, Shocklach Oviatt and Threapwood CPs were transferred to Holt sub-district, and the remaining CPs to WHITCHURCH district).

## INDEX OF SUB-DISTRICTS

| Sub-district | District | Created | Abolished | Registers at |
|---|---|---|---|---|
| Alderley | Macclesfield | 1 Jul 1837 | 1 Apr 1937 | Birkenhead |
| Altrincham | Altrincham | 1 Jul 1837 | 1 Oct 1898 | Trafford |
| Altrincham | Bucklow | 1 Oct 1898 | 1 Apr 1974 | Trafford |
| Bebington | Wirral | 1 Dec 1892 | 1 Apr 1937 | Birkenhead |
| Birkenhead | Birkenhead | 1 Aug 1861 | 1 Apr 1937 | Birkenhead |
| Birkenhead | Wirral | 1 July 1837 | 1 Aug 1861 | Birkenhead |
| Birkenhead North | Birkenhead | 1 Apr 1937 | 1 Apr 1974 | Birkenhead |
| Birkenhead South | Birkenhead | 1 Apr 1937 | 1 Apr 1974 | Birkenhead |
| Bollington | Macclesfield | 1 July 1837 | 1 Apr 1937 | Macclesfield |
| Bredbury | NE Cheshire | 1 Apr 1937 | 1 Apr 1969 | Stockport |
| Bredbury | Stockport | 1 Jun 1905 | 1 Apr 1937 | Stockport |
| Budworth | Runcorn | 1 July 1837 | 1 Apr 1937 | Warrington |
| Bunbury | Nantwich | 1 July 1837 | 1 Mar 1915 | South Cheshire |
| Cheadle | NE Cheshire | 1 Apr 1937 | 1 Apr 1974 | Stockport |
| Cheadle | Stockport | 1 July 1837 | 1 Apr 1937 | Stockport |
| Chester | Chester | 1 Apr 1937 | 1 Apr 1974 | Chester |
| Chester Castle | Chester | 1 Jan 1870 | 1 July 1918 | Chester |
| Chester Castle | Gt. Boughton | 1 July 1837 | 1 Jan 1870 | Chester |
| Chester Castle | West Cheshire | 1 Apr 1937 | 1 Apr 1974 | Chester |
| Chester Cathedral | Chester | 1 Jan 1870 | 1 July 1918 | Chester |
| Chester Cathedral | Gt. Boughton | 1 July 1837 | 1 Jan 1870 | Chester |
| Chester City | Chester | 1 July 1918 | 1 Apr 1937 | Chester |
| Chester Rural | Chester | 1 July 1918 | 1 Apr 1937 | Chester |
| Church Hulme | Congleton | 1 July 1837 | 1 Apr 1937 | South Cheshire |
| Clatterbridge | Wirral | 1 Oct 1959 | 1 Apr 1974 | Birkenhead |
| Congleton | Congleton | 1 July 1837 | 1 Apr 1937 | South Cheshire |
| Congleton | Macclesfield | 1 Apr 1937 | 1 Apr 1974 | South Cheshire |
| Crewe | Crewe | 1 Apr 1937 | 1 Apr 1974 | South Cheshire |
| Crewe | Nantwich | 1 July 1882 | 1 July 1920 | South Cheshire |
| Crewe Borough | Nantwich | 1 July 1920 | 1 Apr 1937 | South Cheshire |
| Daresbury | Runcorn | 6 Oct 1845 | 1 Aug 1891 | Halton |
| Dukinfield | Ashton-u-Lyne | 1 July 1837 | 1 Apr 1897 | Tameside |
| Dukinfield | Ashton-u-Lyne | 1 Aug 1911 | 1 Apr 1937 | Tameside |
| Dukinfield | Hyde | 1 Apr 1937 | 1 Apr 1969 | Tameside |
| Dukinfield & Stalybridge | Hyde | 1 Apr 1969 | 1 Apr 1974 | Tameside |
| Eastham | Wirral | 1 July 1837 | 1 Apr 1937 | Chester |
| East Macclesfield | Macclesfield | 1 July 1837 | 1 Apr 1907 | Macclesfield |
| East Wirral | Wirral | 1 Apr 1937 | 1 Apr 1974 | Birkenhead |

| Sub-district | District | Created | Abolished | Registers at |
|---|---|---|---|---|
| Frodsham | Runcorn | 1 July 1837 | 1 Apr 1937 | Halton |
| Gawsworth | Macclesfield | 1 July 1837 | 1 Apr 1937 | Macclesfield |
| Grappenhall | Runcorn | 1 July 1837 | 6 Oct 1845 | Halton |
| Great Boughton | Chester | 1 Jan 1870 | 1 Aug 1871 | Chester |
| Haslington | Nantwich | 1 July 1920 | 1 Apr 1937 | South Cheshire |
| Hawarden | Chester | 1 Jan 1870 | 1 Jan 1903 | Chester |
| Hawarden | Gt. Boughton | 1 July 1837 | 1 Jan 1870 | Chester |
| Hayfield | Hayfield | 1 July 1837 | 1 Apr 1937 | High Peak |
| Hazel Grove | NE Cheshire | 1 Apr 1937 | 1 Apr 1974 | Stockport |
| Hazel Grove | Stockport | 1 July 1837 | 1 Apr 1937 | Stockport |
| Heaton Norris | Stockport | 1 July 1837 | 1 Apr 1937 | Stockport |
| Holt | Wrexham | 15 May 1853 | 1 Jan 1897 | Wrexham Maelor |
| Hyde | Stockport | 1 July 1837 | 1 Apr 1937 | Tameside |
| Hyde | Hyde | 1 Apr 1937 | 1 Apr 1974 | Tameside |
| Knutsford | Altrincham | 1 July 1837 | 1 Sep 1898 | Macclesfield |
| Knutsford | Bucklow | 1 Sep 1898 | 1 Apr 1974 | Macclesfield |
| Latchford | Warrington | 6 Oct 1845 | 1 Nov 1896 | Warrington |
| Lymm | Altrincham | 1 July 1837 | 1 Sep 1898 | Warrington |
| Lymm | Bucklow | 1 Sep 1898 | 1 Apr 1937 | Warrington |
| Lymm | Bucklow | 1 Apr 1962 | 1 Apr 1974 | Warrington |
| Macclesfield | Macclesfield | 1 Apr 1907 | 1 Apr 1937 | Macclesfield |
| Macclesfield | Macclesfield | 1 Apr 1937 | 1 Oct 1948 | Macclesfield |
| Macclesfield & Bollington | Macclesfield | 1 Oct 1948 | 1 Apr 1974 | Macclesfield |
| Macclesfield Rural | Macclesfield | 1 Oct 1948 | 1 Apr 1974 | Macclesfield |
| Malpas | Wrexham | 1 July 1837 | 15 May 1853 | Wrexham Maelor |
| Malpas | Whitchurch | 1 Nov 1857 | 1 Apr 1937 | Chester |
| Marple | Stockport | 1 July 1837 | 1 June 1905 | Stockport |
| Marple | Stockport | 1 Oct 1923 | 1 Apr 1937 | Stockport |
| Middlewich | Northwich | 1 July 1837 | 1 Apr 1937 | Vale Royal |
| Moreton Say | Mkt. Drayton | 1 July 1837 | 1 Oct 1894 | North Shropshire |
| Mottram | Ashton-u-Lyne | 1 July 1837 | 1 Apr 1937 | Tameside |
| Nantwich | Nantwich | 1 July 1837 | 1 Apr 1937 | South Cheshire |
| Nantwich | Crewe | 1 Apr 1937 | 1 Apr 1974 | South Cheshire |
| Neston | Wirral | 1 July 1837 | 1 Apr 1937 | Birkenhead |
| Newton | Ashton-u-lyne | 1 July 1837 | 1 Oct 1923 | Tameside |
| Newton | Stockport | 1 Oct 1923 | 1 Apr 1937 | Tameside |
| Northwich | Northwich | 1 July 1837 | 1 Apr 1974 | Vale Royal |
| Over | Northwich | 1 July 1837 | 1 Apr 1937 | Vale Royal |
| Prestbury | Macclesfield | 1 July 1837 | 1 Apr 1937 | Macclesfield |

| Sub-district | District | Created | Abolished | Registers at |
|---|---|---|---|---|
| Rainow | Macclesfield | 1 July 1837 | 1 Apr 1928 | Macclesfield |
| Runcorn | Runcorn | 1 July 1837 | 1 Apr 1974 | Halton |
| Sale | Bucklow | 1 Apr 1903 | 1 Apr 1974 | Trafford |
| Sandbach | Congleton | 1 July 1837 | 1 Apr 1937 | South Cheshire |
| Sandbach | Crewe | 1 Apr 1937 | 1 Apr 1974 | South Cheshire |
| Stalybridge | Ashton-u-Lyne | 1 Apr 1897 | 1 Apr 1937 | Tameside |
| Stalybridge | Hyde | 1 Apr 1937 | 1 Apr 1969 | Tameside |
| Stayley | Ashton-u-Lyne | 1 July 1837 | 1 Jan 1883 | Tameside |
| Stockport First | Stockport | 1 July 1837 | 1 Apr 1974 | Stockport |
| Stockport Second | Stockport | 1 July 1837 | 1 Apr 1974 | Stockport |
| Stockport Third | Stockport | 1 Jan 1903 | 1 Apr 1974 | Stockport |
| Stockton Heath | Runcorn | 1 Apr 1937 | 1 Apr 1974 | Warrington |
| Sutton | Macclesfield | 1 July 1837 | 1 Dec 1910 | Macclesfield |
| Tarvin Rural | West Cheshire | 1 Apr 1937 | 1 Apr 1974 | Chester |
| Tattenhall | Chester | 1 Jan 1870 | 1 Apr 1937 | Chester |
| Tattenhall | Gt. Boughton | 1 July 1837 | 1 Jan 1870 | Chester |
| Tranmere | Birkenhead | 1 Aug 1861 | 1 Apr 1937 | Birkenhead |
| Wallasey | Wirral | 1 July 1837 | 1 Aug 1861 | Wallasey |
| Wallasey | Birkenhead | 1 Aug 1861 | 1 Apr 1936 | Wallasey |
| Wallasey | Wallasey | 1 Apr 1936 | 1 Apr 1974 | Wallasey |
| Weaverham | Northwich | 1 July 1837 | 1 Apr 1937 | Vale Royal |
| West Macc'field | Macclesfield | 1 July 1837 | 1 Apr 1907 | Macclesfield |
| West Wirral | Wirral | 1 Apr 1937 | 1 Apr 1974 | Birkenhead |
| Whitchurch | Whitchurch | 1 Apr 1853 | 1 Apr 1937 | North Shropshire |
| Wimslow | Altrincham | 1 July 1837 | 1 Sep 1898 | Macclesfield |
| Wilmslow | Bucklow | 1 Sep 1898 | 1 Apr 1974 | Macclesfield |
| Winsford | Northwich | 1 Apr 1937 | 1 Apr 1974 | Vale Royal |
| Woodchurch | Wirral | 1 July 1837 | 1 Apr 1937 | Birkenhead |
| Wrenbury | Nantwich | 1 July 1837 | 1 Apr 1937 | South Cheshire |
| Wybunbury | Nantwich | 1 July 1837 | 1 July 1882 | South Cheshire |

# INDEX OF CIVIL PARISHES

Showing the names of the Registration Districts in which they were situated (names of sub-districts are shown in parentheses).

| | |
|---|---|
| Acton (nr. Nantwich) | 1837-1937: Nantwich (Nantwich); 1937-74: Crewe (Nantwich); 1974-88:Congleton & Crewe; from 1988: South Cheshire. |
| Acton (nr. Weaverham) | 1837-1967: Northwich (Weaverham, Northwich); from 1967: see Acton Bridge CP. |
| Acton Bridge | 1837-1967: see Acton CP; 1967-74: Northwich (Northwich); from 1974: Vale Royal. |
| Acton Grange | 1837-1936: Runcorn (Grappenhall, Daresbury, Budworth); from 1936: see Walton CP. |
| Adlington | 1837-1974: Macclesfield (Prestbury, Macclesfield, Macclesfield Rural); from 1974: Macclesfield. |
| Agden (nr. Lymm) | 1837-98: Altrincham (Lymm); 1898-1974: Bucklow (Lymm, Knutsford, Lymm); from 1974: Macclesfield. |
| Agden (nr. Malpas) | 1837-53: Wrexham (Malpas); 1853-1937: Whitchurch (Whitchurch, Malpas); 1937-74: West Cheshire (Tarvin Rural); from 1974: Chester & Ellesmere Port. |
| Alderley | See Nether Alderley, Over Alderley CPs. |
| Alderley Edge | 1837-94: see Chorley CP; 1894-1937: Macclesfield (Alderley); 1936-74: Bucklow (Wilmslow); from 1974: Macclesfield. |
| Aldersey | 1837-69: Great Boughton (Tattenhall); 1870-1937: Chester (Tattenhall); 1937-74: West Cheshire (Tarvin Rural); from 1974: Chester & Ellesmere Port. |
| Aldford | 1837-69: Great Boughton (Tattenhall); 1870-1937: Chester (Tattenhall); 1937-74: West Cheshire (Chester Castle); from 1974: Chester & Ellesmere Port. |
| Allostock | 1837-1974: Northwich (Northwich); from 1974: Vale Royal. |
| Alpraham | 1837-1937: Nantwich (Bunbury, Wrenbury); 1937-74: Crewe (Nantwich); 1974-88: Congleton & Crewe; from 1988: South Cheshire. |
| Alsager | 1837-1937: Congleton (Sandbach); 1937-74: Crewe (Sandbach); 1974-88: Congleton & Crewe; from 1988: South Cheshire. |
| Altrincham | 1837-98: Altrincham (Altrincham); 1898-1974: Bucklow (Altrincham); from 1974: Trafford [Gtr. Man.]. |
| Alvanley | 1837-1974: Runcorn (Frodsham, Runcorn); from 1974: Vale Royal. |

| | |
|---|---|
| Alvaston | 1837-99: Nantwich (Nantwich); from 1899 see Worleston CP. |
| Anderton | 1837-1974: Northwich (Northwich); from 1974: Vale Royal. |
| Antrobus | 1837-1974: Runcorn (Budworth, Stockton Heath); from 1974: Vale Royal. |
| Appleton | 1837-1974: Runcorn (Budworth, Stockton Heath); from 1974: Vale Royal. |
| Arclid | 1837-1937: Congleton (Sandbach); 1937-74: Crewe (Sandbach); 1974-88: Congleton & Crewe; from 1988: South Cheshire. |
| Arrowe | 1837-1933: Wirral (Woodchurch); from 1933: see Birkenhead, Irby CPs. |
| Ashley | 1837-98: Altrincham (Altrincham); 1898-74: Bucklow (Altrincham); from 1974: Macclesfield. |
| Ashton | 1837-69: Great Boughton (Chester Castle Division); 1870-1937: Chester (Great Boughton, Tattenhall); 1937-74: West Cheshire (Tarvin Rural); from 1974: Chester & Ellesmere Port. |
| Ashton upon Mersey | 1837-98: Altrincham (Altrincham); 1898-1936: Bucklow (Altrincham, Sale); from 1936: see Sale CP. |
| Astbury | See Newbold Astbury CP. |
| Aston | 1837-1936: see Aston by Sutton, Aston Grange CPs; 1936-74: Runcorn (Runcorn); from 1974: Vale Royal. |
| Aston by Budworth | 1837-98: Altrincham (Lymm); 1898-1974: Bucklow (Lymm, Knutsford); from 1974: Macclesfield. |
| Aston by Sutton | 1837-1936: Runcorn (Runcorn); from 1936: see Aston CP. |
| Aston Grange | 1837-1936: Runcorn (Runcorn); from 1936: see Aston CP. |
| Aston juxta Mondrum | 1837-1937: Nantwich (Nantwich); 1937-74: Crewe (Nantwich); 1974-88: Congleton & Crewe; from 1988: South Cheshire. |
| Audlem | 1837-1937: Nantwich (Wrenbury); 1937-74: Crewe (Nantwich); 1974-88: Congleton & Crewe; from 1988: South Cheshire. |
| Austerson | 1837-1937: Nantwich (Nantwich); 1937-74: Crewe (Nantwich); 1974-88: Congleton & Crewe; from 1988: South Cheshire. |
| Bache | 1837-69: Great Boughton (Chester Cathedral Division); 1870-1937: Chester (Great Boughton, Chester Cathedral, Chester Rural); 1937-74: West Cheshire (Chester Castle); from 1974: Chester & Ellesmere Port. |

| | |
|---|---|
| Backford | 1837-69: Great Boughton (Chester Cathedral Division); 1870-1937: Chester (Great Boughton, Chester Cathedral, Chester Rural); 1937-74: West Cheshire (Chester Castle); from 1974: Chester & Ellesmere Port. |
| Baddiley | 1837-1937: Nantwich (Wrenbury, Nantwich); 1937-74: Crewe (Nantwich); 1974-88: Congleton & Crewe; from 1988: South Cheshire. |
| Baddington | 1837-1937: Nantwich (Nantwich); 1937-74: Crewe (Nantwich); 1974-88: Congleton & Crewe; from 1988: South Cheshire. |
| Baguley | 1837-98: Altrincham (Altrincham); 1898-1931: Bucklow (Altrincham, Sale); from 1931: see Manchester CP [*Lancs.*]. |
| Barnston | 1837-1974: Wirral (Woodchurch, Brimstage, East Wirral); from 1974: Birkenhead [*Mers.*]. |
| Barnton | 1837-1974: Northwich (Weaverham, Northwich); from 1974: Vale Royal. |
| Barrow | 1837-69: Great Boughton (Chester Castle Division); 1870-1937: Chester (Great Boughton, Tattenhall); 1937-74: West Cheshire (Chester Castle); from 1974: Chester & Ellesmere Port. |
| Barthomley | 1837-1937: Nantwich (Wybunbury, Crewe, Haslington); 1937-74: Crewe (Crewe); 1974-88: Congleton & Crewe; from 1988: South Cheshire. |
| Bartington | 1837-1936: Runcorn (Budworth); from 1936: see Dutton CP. |
| Barton | 1837-69: Great Boughton (Tattenhall); 1870-1937: Chester (Tattenhall); 1937-74: West Cheshire (Tarvin Rural); from 1974: Chester & Ellesmere Port. |
| Basford | 1837-1937: Nantwich (Wybunbury, Crewe, Haslington); 1937-74: Crewe (Crewe); 1974-88: Congleton & Crewe; from 1988: South Cheshire. |
| Batherton | 1837-1937: Nantwich (Wybunbury, Crewe, Nantwich); 1937-74: Crewe (Nantwich); 1974-88: Congleton & Crewe; from 1988: South Cheshire. |
| Bebington | 1837-1922: see Higher Bebington, Lower Bebington CPs; from 1922: see Bebington cum Bromborough CP. |
| Bebington cum Bromborough | 1837-1922: see Bromborough, Higher Bebington, Lower Bebington CPs; 1922-74: Wirral (Bebington, East Wirral); from 1974: Birkenhead [*in Mers.*] |
| Beeston | 1837-92: Nantwich (Bunbury); 1892-1937: Chester (Tattenhall); 1937-74: West Cheshire (Tarvin Rural); from 1974: Chester & Ellesmere Port. |

| | |
|---|---|
| Betchton | 1837-1937: Congleton (Sandbach); 1937-74: Crewe (Sandbach); 1974-88: Congleton & Crewe; from 1988: South Cheshire. |
| Bexton | 1837-98: Altrincham (Knutsford); 1898-74: Bucklow (Knutsford); from 1974: Macclesfield. |
| Bickerton | 1837-1937: Nantwich (Wrenbury, Bunbury, Wrenbury); 1937-74: Crewe (Nantwich); 1974-88: Congleton & Crewe; from 1988: South Cheshire. |
| Bickley | 1837-53: Nantwich (Wrenbury); 1853-1937: Whitchurch (Whitchurch, Malpas); 1937-74: West Cheshire (Tarvin Rural); from 1974: Chester & Ellesmere Port. |
| Bidston cum Ford | 1837-61: Wirral (Wallasey); 1861-1933: Birkenhead (Tranmere); from 1933: see Birkenhead, Wallasey CP. |
| Birches | 1837-92: Northwich (Northwich); from 1892: see Lach Dennis CP. |
| Birkenhead | 1837-61: Wirral (Birkenhead); 1861-1937: Birkenhead (Birkenhead, Tranmere); 1933-37: Wirral (Woodchurch); 1937-74: Birkenhead (Birkenhead North, Birkenhead South); from 1974: Birkenhead [Mers.]. |
| Birtles | 1837-1936: Macclesfield (Alderley); from 1936: see Henbury CP. |
| Blackden | 1837-1936: Congleton (Church Hulme); from 1936: see Goostrey CP. |
| Blacon cum Crabwall | 1837-69: Great Boughton (Chester Cathedral Division); 1869-1936: Chester (Great Boughton, Chester Cathedral, Chester Rural); from 1936: see Chester, Mollington CPs. |
| Blakenhall | 1837-1937: Nantwich (Wybunbury, Crewe, Nantwich); 1937-74: Crewe (Nantwich); 1974-88: Congleton & Crewe; from 1988: South Cheshire. |
| Bollin Fee | 1837-98: Altrincham (Wilmslow); 1898-36: Bucklow (Wilmslow); from 1936: see Alderley Edge, Wilmslow CPs. |
| Bollington (nr. Lymm) | 1837-98: Altrincham(Lymm); 1898-1974: Bucklow (Lymm, Knustford, Lymm); from 1974: Macclesfield. |
| Bollington (nr. Macclesfield) | 1837-1974: Macclesfield (Bollington, Prestbury, Macclesfield, Macclesfield & Bollington); from 1974: Macclesfield. |
| Bosden | 1837-77: see Handforth cum Bosden CP; 1877-1900: Stockport (Hazel Grove); from 1900: see Hazel Grove cum Bramhall CP. |
| Bosley | 1837-1974: Macclesfield (Gawsworth, Macclesfield, Macclesfield Rural); from 1974: Macclesfield. |

| | |
|---|---|
| Bostock | 1837-1974: Northwich (Middlewich, Winsford); from 1974: Vale Royal. |
| Boughton | See Great Boughton, Spital Boughton CPs. |
| Bowdon | 1837-98: Altrincham (Altrincham); 1898-1974: Bucklow (Altrincham, Lymm, Altrincham); from 1974: Trafford [*Gtr. Man.*] |
| Bradley | 1837-53: Wrexham (Malpas); 1853-1937: Whitchurch (Whitchurch, Malpas); 1937-74: West Cheshire (Tarvin Rural); from 1974: Chester & Ellesmere Port. |
| Bradwall | 1837-1937: Congleton (Sandbach); 1937-74: Crewe (Sandbach); 1974-88: Congleton & Crewe; from 1988: South Cheshire. |
| Bramhall | 1837-1900: Stockport (Hazel Grove); from 1900: see Hazel Grove cum Bramhall CP. |
| Bredbury | 1837-1936: Stockport (Hyde, Stockport Second, Bredbury); from 1936: see Bredbury & Romiley, Marple, Hyde CPs. |
| Bredbury & Romiley | 1837-1936: see Bredbury, Romiley, Compstall, Hyde CPs; 1936-37: Stockport (Bredbury, Hyde); 1937-74: North East Cheshire (Bredbury, Hazel Grove); from 1974: Stockport [*Gtr. Man.*]. |
| Brereton | 1837-1936: see Brereton cum Smethwick, Davenport CPs; 1936-37: Congleton (Church Hulme); 1937-74: Crewe (Sandbach); 1974-88: Congleton & Crewe; from 1988: South Cheshire. |
| Brereton cum Smethwick | 1837-1936: Congleton (Church Hulme); from 1936: see Brereton CP. |
| Bridgemere | 1837-1937: Nantwich (Wybunbury, Crewe, Nantwich); 1937-74: Crewe (Nantwich); 1974-88: Congleton & Crewe; from 1988: South Cheshire. |
| Bridge Trafford | 1837-69: Great Boughton (Chester Cathedral Division); 1870-1937: Chester (Great Boughton, Chester Cathedral, Chester Rural); 1937-74: West Cheshire (Chester Castle); from 1974: Chester & Ellesmere Port |
| Brimstage | 1837-1974: Wirral (Eastham, Bebington, East Wirral); from 1974: Birkenhead [*Mers.*]. |
| Brindley | 1837-1937: Nantwich (Nantwich); 1937-74: Crewe (Nantwich); 1974-88: Congleton & Crewe; from 1988: South Cheshire. |
| Brinnington | 1837-1902: Stockport (Stockport Second); from 1902: see Bredbury, Stockport CPs. |
| Bromborough | 1837-1922: Wirral (Eastham, Bebington); from 1922: see Bebington cum Bromborough CP. |

| | |
|---|---|
| Broomhall | 1837-1937: Nantwich (Wrenbury); 1937-74: Crewe (Nantwich); 1974-88: Congleton & Crewe; from 1988: South Cheshire. |
| Broxton | 1837-69: Great Boughton (Tattenhall); 1870-1937: Chester (Tattenhall); 1937-74: West Cheshire (Tarvin Rural); from 1974: Chester & Ellesmere Port. |
| Bruen Stapleford | 1837-69: Great Boughton (Tattenhall); 1870-1937: Chester (Tattenhall); 1937-74: West Cheshire (Tarvin Rural); from 1974: Chester & Ellesmere Port. |
| Budworth | See Great Budworth, Little Budworth CPs. |
| Buerton (nr. Aldford) | 1837-69: Great Boughton (Tattenhall); 1870-1937: Chester (Tattenhall); 1937-74: West Cheshire (Chester Castle); from 1974: Chester & Ellesmere Port. |
| Buerton (nr. Audlem) | 1837-1937: Nantwich (Wrenbury); 1937-74: Crewe (Nantwich); 1974-88: Congleton & Crewe; from 1988: South Cheshire. |
| Buglawton | 1837-1936: Congleton (Congleton); from 1936: see Congleton, Eaton, North Rode CPs. |
| Bulkeley | 1837-1937: Nantwich (Wrenbury, Bunbury, Wrenbury); 1937-74: Crewe (Nantwich); 1974-88: Congleton & Crewe; from 1988: South Cheshire. |
| Bunbury | 1837-1937: Nantwich (Bunbury, Wrenbury); 1937-74: Crewe (Nantwich); 1974-88: Congleton & Crewe; from 1988: South Cheshire. |
| Burland | 1837-1937: Nantwich (Nantwich); 1937-74: Crewe (Nantwich); 1974-88: Congleton & Crewe; from 1988: South Cheshire. |
| Burton (nr. Neston) | 1837-1974: Wirral (Neston, West Wirral); from 1974: Chester & Ellesmere Port. |
| Burton by Tarvin | 1837-69: Great Boughton (Tattenhall); 1870-1937: Chester (Tattenhall); 1937-74: West Cheshire (Tarvin Rural); from 1974: Chester & Ellesmere Port. |
| Burwardsley | 1837-92: Nantwich (Bunbury); 1892-1937: Chester (Tattenhall); 1937-74: West Cheshire (Tarvin Rural); from 1974: Chester & Ellesmere Port. |
| Butley | 1837-1936: Macclesfield (Prestbury); from 1936: see Prestbury, Bollington CPs. |
| Byley | 1837-1937: Northwich (Middlewich); 1936-1937: Congleton (Church Hulme); 1937-74: Northwich (Winsford); from 1974: Vale Royal. |
| Caldecott | 1837-69: Great Boughton (Tattenhall); 1870-1937: Chester (Tattenhall); 1937-74: West Cheshire (Tarvin Rural); from 1974: Chester & Ellesmere Port. |

| | |
|---|---|
| Caldy | 1837-1974: Wirral (Woodchurch, West Wirral); from 1974: Birkenhead [*Mers.*]. |
| Calveley | 1837-1937: Nantwich (Wrenbury, Bunbury); 1937-74: Crewe (Nantwich); 1974-88: Congleton & Crewe; from 1988: South Cheshire. |
| Capenhurst | 1837-69: Great Boughton (Chester Cathedral Division); 1870-1937: Chester (Great Boughton, Chester Cathedral, Chester Rural); 1937-74: West Cheshire (Chester Castle); from 1974: Chester & Ellesmere Port. |
| Capesthorne | 1837-1936: Macclesfield (Alderley); from 1936: see Siddington CP. |
| Carden | 1837-69: Great Boughton (Tattenhall); 1870-1937: Chester (Tattenhall); 1937-74: West Cheshire (Tarvin Rural); from 1974: Chester & Ellesmere Port. |
| Carrington | 1837-98: Altrincham (Altrincham); 1898-1974: Bucklow (Altrincham, Sale); from 1974: Trafford [*Gtr. Man.*]. |
| Castle Northwich | 1837-94: Northwich (Northwich); from 1894: see Northwich. |
| Cathedral Precincts | 1837-69: Great Boughton (Chester Cathedral Division); 1870-1884: Chester (Chester Cathedral); from 1884: see Chester. |
| Caughall | 1837-69: Great Boughton (Chester Cathedral Division); 1870-1937: Chester (Great Boughton, Chester Cathedral, Chester Rural); 1937-74: West Cheshire (Chester Castle); from 1974: Chester & Ellesmere Port. |
| Cheadle | 1837-79: see Cheadle Bulkeley, Cheadle Moseley CPs; 1879-1930: Stockport (Cheadle, Stockport First); from 1930: see Cheadle & Gatley CP. |
| Cheadle & Gatley | 1837-1930: see Cheadle, Cheadle Bulkeley, Cheadle Moseley, Stockport Etchells CPs; 1930-1937: Stockport (Cheadle); 1937-74: North East Cheshire (Cheadle); from 1974: Stockport [*Gtr. Man.*]. |
| Cheadle Bulkeley | 1837-79: Stockport (Cheadle, Stockport First); from 1879: see Cheadle CP. |
| Cheadle Moseley | 1837-79: Stockport (Cheadle, Stockport First); from 1879: see Cheadle CP. |
| Checkley cum Wrinehill | 1837-1937: Nantwich (Wybunbury, Crewe, Nantwich); 1937-74: Crewe (Nantwich); 1974-88: Congleton & Crewe; from 1988: South Cheshire. |
| Chelford | 1837-1974: Macclesfield (Alderley, Macclesfield, Macclesfield Rural); from1974: Macclesfield. |

| | |
|---|---|
| Chester | 1837-84: see Cathedral Precincts, Holy Trinity, St. Bridget, St. John the Baptist, St. Martin, St. Mary on the Hill, St. Michael, St. Olave, St. Oswald, St. Peter, Spital Boughton CPs; 1884-1974: Chester (Chester Castle, Chester Cathedral, Chester City, Chester Rural, Chester); from 1974: Chester & Ellesmere Port. |
| Chester Castle | 1837-69: Great Boughton (Chester Castle Division); 1870-1937: Chester (Chester Castle, Chester Rural); 1937-74: West Cheshire (Chester Castle); from 1974: Chester & Ellesmere Port. |
| Chidlow | 1837-53: Wrexham (Malpas); 1853-1937: Whitchurch (Whitchurch, Malpas); 1937-74: West Cheshire (Tarvin Rural); from 1974: Chester & Ellesmere Port. |
| Childer Thornton | 1837-1937: Wirral (Eastham, Neston); 1937-50: West Cheshire (Chester Castle); from 1950: see Ellesmere Port CP. |
| Cholmondeley | 1837-1937: Nantwich (Wrenbury, Bunbury, Wrenbury); 1937-74: Crewe (Nantwich); 1974-88: Congleton & Crewe; from 1988: South Cheshire. |
| Cholmondeston | 1837-1937: Nantwich (Nantwich); 1937-74: Crewe (Nantwich); 1974-88: Congleton & Crewe; from 1988: South Cheshire. |
| Chorley (nr. Alderley | 1837-1974: Macclesfield (Alderley, Macclesfield, Edge) Macclesfield Rural); from 1974: Macclesfield |
| Chorley (nr. Nantwich) | 1837-1937: Nantwich (Wrenbury); 1937-74: Crewe (Nantwich); 1974-88: Congleton & Crewe; from 1988: South Cheshire. |
| Chorlton (nr. Crewe) | 1837-1937: Nantwich (Wybunbury, Crewe, Nantwich); 1937-74: Crewe (Nantwich); 1974-88: Congleton & Crewe; from 1988: South Cheshire. |
| Chorlton (nr. Malpas) | 1837-53: Wrexham (Malpas); 1853-1937: Whitchurch (Whitchurch, Malpas); 1937-74: West Cheshire (Tarvin Rural); from 1974: Chester & Ellesmere Port. |
| Chorlton by Backford | 1837-69: Great Boughton (Chester Cathedral Division); 1870-1937: Chester (Great Boughton, Chester Cathedral, Chester Rural); 1937-74: West Cheshire (Chester Castle); from 1974: Chester & Ellesmere Port. |
| Chowley | 1837-69: Great Boughton (Tattenhall); 1870-1937: Chester (Tattenhall); 1937-74: West Cheshire (Tarvin Rural); from 1974: Chester & Ellesmere Port. |

| | |
|---|---|
| Christleton | 1837-69: Great Boughton (Chester Cathedral Division); 1870-1937: Chester (Great Boughton, Chester Cathedral, Chester Rural); 1937-74: West Cheshire (Chester Castle); from 1974: Chester & Ellesmere Port. |
| Church Coppenhall | 1837-1936: Nantwich (Wybunbury, Crewe, Haslington); from 1936: see Monks Coppenhall CP. |
| Church Hulme | 1837-1937: Congleton (Church Hulme); 1937-74: Crewe (Sandbach); 1974-88: Congleton & Crewe; from 1988: South Cheshire. |
| Church Lawton | 1837-1937: Congleton (Church Hulme); 1937-74: Crewe (Sandbach); 1974-88: Congleton & Crewe; from 1988: South Cheshire. |
| Church Minshull | 1837-1937: Nantwich (Bunbury, Nantwich); 1937-74: Crewe (Nantwich); 1974-88: Congleton & Crewe; from 1988: South Cheshire. |
| Church Shocklach | 1837-97: Wrexham (Malpas, Holt); 1897-1937: Chester (Tattenhall); 1937-74: West Cheshire (Tarvin Rural); from 1974: Chester & Ellesmere Port. |
| Churton by Aldford | 1837-69: Great Boughton (Tattenhall); 1870-1937: Chester (Tattenhall); 1937-74: West Cheshire (Tarvin Rural); from 1974: Chester & Ellesmere Port. |
| Churton by Farndon | 1837-69: Great Boughton (Tattenhall); 1870-1937: Chester (Tattenhall); 1937-74: West Cheshire (Tarvin Rural); from 1974: Chester & Ellesmere Port. |
| Churton Heath | 1837-69: Great Boughton (Tattenhall); 1870-1937: Chester (Tattenhall); 1937-74: West Cheshire (Chester Castle); from 1974: Chester & Ellesmere Port. |
| Claughton with Grange | 1837-61: Wirral (Wallasey); 1861-98: Birkenhead (Tranmere); from 1898: see Birkenhead CP. |
| Claverton | 1837-69: Great Boughton (Hawarden); 1870-1937: Chester (Hawarden, Chester Castle, Chester Rural); 1937-74: West Cheshire (Chester Castle); from 1974: Chester & Ellesmere Port. |
| Clifton | 1837-1936: Runcorn (Runcorn); from 1936: see Sutton, Runcorn CPs. |
| Clive | 1837-1936: Northwich (Over); from 1936: see Winsford CP. |
| Clotton Hoofield | 1837-69: Great Boughton (Tattenhall); 1870-1937: Chester (Tattenhall); 1937-74: West Cheshire (Tarvin Rural); from 1974: Chester & Ellesmere Port. |
| Clutton | 1837-69: Great Boughton (Tattenhall); 1870-1937: Chester (Tattenhall); 1937-74: West Cheshire (Tarvin Rural); from 1974: Chester & Ellesmere Port. |

| | |
|---|---|
| Coddington | 1837-69: Great Boughton (Tattenhall); 1870-1937: Chester (Tattenhall); 1937-74: West Cheshire (Tarvin Rural); from 1974: Chester & Ellesmere Port. |
| Cogshall | 1837-1936: Northwich (Northwich); from 1936: see Comberbach CP. |
| Comberbach | 1837-1974: Northwich (Northwich); from 1974: Vale Royal. |
| Compstall | 1837-97: see Werneth CP; 1897-1936: Stockport (Hyde, Bredbury); from 1936: see Bredbury & Romiley and Hyde CPs. |
| Congleton | 1837-1937: Congleton (Congleton); 1937-74: Macclesfield (Crewe); 1974-88: Congleton & Crewe; from 1988: South Cheshire. |
| Coole Pilate | 1837-1937: Nantwich (Nantwich, Wrenbury); 1937-74: Crewe (Nantwich); 1974-88: Congleton & Crewe; from 1988: South Cheshire. |
| Coppenhall | See Church Coppenhall, Monks Coppenhall CPs. |
| Cotton | 1837-1936: Congleton (Church Hulme); from 1936: see Cranage CP. |
| Cotton Abbotts | 1837-69: Great Boughton (Chester Castle Division); 1870-1937: Chester (Great Boughton, Tattenhall); 1937-74: West Cheshire (Tarvin Rural); from 1974: Chester & Ellesmere Port. |
| Cotton Edmunds | 1837-69: Great Boughton (Chester Castle Division); 1870-1937: Chester (Great Boughton, Tattenhall); 1937-74: West Cheshire (Tarvin Rural); from 1974: Chester & Ellesmere Port. |
| Cranage | 1837-1937: Congleton (Church Hulme); 1937-74: Crewe (Sandbach); 1974-88: Congleton & Crewe; from 1988: South Cheshire. |
| Crewe (Borough) | See Monks Coppenhall CP. |
| Crewe (Green) | 1837-1936: Nantwich (Wybunbury, Crewe, Haslington); 1937-74: Crewe (Crewe); 1974-88: Congleton & Crewe; from 1988: South Cheshire. |
| Crewe by Farndon | 1837-69: Great Boughton (Tattenhall); 1870-1937: Chester (Tattenhall); 1937-74: West Cheshire (Tarvin Rural); from 1974: Chester & Ellesmere Port. |
| Croughton | 1837-69: Great Boughton (Chester Cathedral Division); 1870-1937: Chester (Great Boughton, Chester Cathedral, Chester Rural); 1937-74: West Cheshire (Chester Castle); from 1974: Chester & Ellesmere Port. |
| Crowley | 1837-1936: Runcorn (Budworth); from 1936: see Antrobus CP. |

| | |
|---|---|
| Crowton | 1837-1974: Northwich (Weaverham, Northwich); from 1974: Vale Royal. |
| Croxton | 1837-92: Northwich (Middlewich); from 1892: see Byley CP. |
| Cuddington (nr. Malpas) | 1837-53: Wrexham (Malpas); 1853-1937: Whitchurch (Whitchurch, Malpas); 1937-74: West Cheshire (Tarvin Rural); from 1974: Chester & Ellesmere Port. |
| Cuddington (nr. Weaverham) | 1837-1974: Northwich (Weaverham, Northwich); from 1974: Vale Royal. |
| Daresbury | 1837-1974: Runcorn (Grappenhall, Daresbury, Budworth, Stockton Heath); from 1974: Halton. |
| Darnhall | 1837-1974: Northwich (Over, Winsford); from 1974: Vale Royal. |
| Davenham | 1837-1974: Northwich (Middlewich, Winsford); from 1974: Vale Royal. |
| Davenport | 1837-1936: Congleton (Church Hulme); from 1936: see Brereton CP. |
| Delamere | 1837-1974: Northwich (Weaverham, Winsford); from 1974: Vale Royal. |
| Disley | 1837-1937: Hayfield (Hayfield); 1936-37: Macclesfield (Bollington); 1937-74: North East Cheshire (Hazel Grove); from 1974: Macclesfield. |
| Dodcott cum Wilkesley | 1837-1937: Nantwich (Wrenbury); 1937-74: Crewe (Nantwich); 1974-88: Congleton & Crewe; from 1988: South Cheshire. |
| Doddington | 1837-1937: Nantwich (Wybunbury, Crewe, Nantwich); 1937-74: Crewe (Nantwich); 1974-88: Congleton & Crewe; from 1988: South Cheshire. |
| Dodleston | 1837-69: Great Boughton (Hawarden); 1870-1937: Chester (Hawarden, Chester Castle, Chester Rural); 1937-74: West Cheshire (Chester Castle); from 1974: Chester & Ellesmere Port. |
| Duckington | 1837-53: Great Boughton (Tattenhall); 1853-1937: Whitchurch (Whitchurch, Malpas); 1937-74: West Cheshire (Tarvin Rural); from 1974: Chester & Ellesmere Port. |
| Duddon | 1837-69: Great Boughton (Tattenhall); 1870-1937: Chester (Tattenhall); 1937-74: West Cheshire (Tarvin Rural); from 1974: Chester & Ellesmere Port. |
| Dukinfield | 1837-1937: Ashton under Lyne (Dukinfield, Stalybridge); 1936-37: Stockport (Hyde); 1937-74: Hyde (Dukinfield, Dukinfield & Stalybridge); from 1974: Tameside [*Gtr. Man.*]. |

| | |
|---|---|
| Dunham Massey | 1837-98: Altrincham (Altrincham); 1898-1974: Bucklow (Altrincham); from 1974: Trafford [*Gtr. Man.*]. |
| Dunham on the Hill | 1837-69: Great Boughton (Chester Cathedral Division); 1870-1937: Chester (Great Boughton, Chester Cathedral, Chester Rural); 1937-74: West Cheshire (Chester Castle); from 1974: Chester & Ellesmere Port. |
| Dutton | 1837-1974: Runcorn (Grappenhall, Daresbury, Budworth, Stockton Heath); from 1974: Vale Royal. |
| Eastham | 1837-1974: Wirral (Eastham, East Wirral); from 1974: Birkenhead [*Mers.*]. |
| Eaton (nr. Chester) | 1837-69: Great Boughton (Hawarden); 1870-1937: Chester (Hawarden, Chester Castle, Chester Rural); 1937-74: West Cheshire (Chester Castle); from 1974: Chester & Ellesmere Port. |
| Eaton (nr. Macclesfield) | 1837-1974: Macclesfield (Gawsworth, Macclesfield, Macclesfield Rural); from 1974: Macclesfield |
| Eaton (nr. Northwich) | 1837-1936: Northwich (Over); from 1936: see Davenham, Winsford, Hartford CPs. |
| Eaton (nr. Tarporley) | 1837-1892: Nantwich (Bunbury); 1892-1936: Chester (Tattenhall); from 1936: see Rushton, Utkinton, Tarporley CPs. |
| Eccleston | 1837-69: Great Boughton (Hawarden); 1870-1937: Chester (Hawarden, Chester Castle, Chester Rural); 1937-74: West Cheshire (Chester Castle); from 1974: Chester & Ellesmere Port. |
| Eddisbury | 1837-1936: Northwich (Weaverham); from 1936: see Delamere CP. |
| Edge | 1837-53: Great Boughton (Tattenhall); 1853-1937: Whitchurch (Whitchurch, Malpas); 1937-74: West Cheshire (Tarvin Rural); from 1974: Chester & Ellesmere Port. |
| Edgerley | 1837-69: Great Boughton (Tattenhall); 1870-1937: Chester (Tattenhall); 1937-74: West Cheshire (Tarvin Rural); from 1974: Chester & Ellesmere Port. |
| Edleston | 1837-1937: Nantwich (Nantwich); 1937-74: Crewe (Nantwich); 1974-88: Congleton & Crewe; from 1988: South Cheshire. |
| Egerton | 1837-1937: Nantwich (Wrenbury, Bunbury, Wrenbury); 1937-74: Crewe (Nantwich); 1974-88: Congleton & Crewe; from 1988: South Cheshire. |
| Ellesmere Port | 1837-1911: see Netherpool, Overpool, Whitby CPs; 1911-37: Wirral (Eastham); 1937-74: West Cheshire (Chester Castle); from 1974: Chester & Ellesmere Port. |

| | |
|---|---|
| Elton (nr. Chester) | 1837-69: Great Boughton (Chester Cathedral Division); 1870-1937: Chester (Great Boughton, Chester Cathedral, Chester Rural); 1937-74: West Cheshire (Chester Castle); from 1974: Chester & Ellesmere Port. |
| Elton (nr. Sandbach) | 1837-1937: Congleton (Sandbach); 1937-70: Crewe (Sandbach); from 1970: see Moston CP. |
| Etchells | See Northen Etchells, Stockport Etchells CPs. |
| Faddiley | 1837-1937: Nantwich (Nantwich); 1937-74: Crewe (Nantwich); 1974-88: Congleton & Crewe; from 1988: South Cheshire. |
| Fallibroome | 1837-1936: Macclesfield (Prestbury); from 1936: see Prestbury, Macclesfield CPs. |
| Farndon | 1837-69: Great Boughton (Tattenhall); 1870-1937: Chester (Tattenhall); 1937-74: West Cheshire (Tarvin Rural); from 1974: Chester & Ellesmere Port. |
| Foulk Stapleford | 1837-69: Great Boughton (Tattenhall); 1870-1937: Chester (Tattenhall); 1937-74: West Cheshire (Tarvin Rural); from 1974: Chester & Ellesmere Port. |
| Frankby | 1837-1974: Wirral (Woodchurch, West Wirral); from 1974: Birkenhead [*Mers*]. |
| Frodsham | 1837-1974: Runcorn (Frodsham, Runcorn); from 1974: Vale Royal. |
| Frodsham Lordship | 1837-1936: Runcorn (Frodsham); from 1936: see Frodsham CP. |
| Fulshaw | 1837-1894: Altrincham (Wilmslow); from 1894: see Wilmslow, Bollin Fee CPs. |
| Gatley | 1837-1930: see Stockport Etchells CP; from 1930: see Cheadle & Gatley CP. |
| Gawsworth | 1837-1974: Macclesfield (Gawsworth, Macclesfield, Macclesfield Rural); from 1974: Macclesfield. |
| Gayton | 1837-1974: Wirral (Neston, West Wirral); from 1974: Birkenhead [*Mers.*]. |
| Godley | 1837-1923: Ashton-under-Lyne (Newton); from 1923: see Hyde CP. |
| Golborne Bellow | 1837-69: Great Boughton (Tattenhall); 1870-1937: Chester (Tattenhall); 1937-74: West Cheshire (Tarvin Rural); from 1974: Chester & Ellesmere Port. |
| Golborne David | 1837-69: Great Boughton (Tattenhall); 1870-1937: Chester (Tattenhall); 1937-74: West Cheshire (Tarvin Rural); from 1974: Chester & Ellesmere Port. |

| | |
|---|---|
| Goostrey | 1837-1936: see Goostrey cum Barnshaw, Blackden CPs; 1936-37: Congleton (Church Hulme); 1937-74: Crewe (Sandbach); 1974-88: Congleton & Crewe; from 1988: South Cheshire. |
| Goostrey cum Barnshaw | 1837-1936: Congleton (Church Hulme); from 1936: see Goostrey CP. |
| Grafton | 1837-69: Great Boughton (Tattenhall); 1870-1937: Chester (Tattenhall); 1937-74: West Cheshire (Tarvin Rural); from 1974: Chester & Ellesmere Port. |
| Grange | 1837-1974: Wirral (Woodchurch, West Wirral); from 1974: Birkenhead [Mers.]. |
| Grappenhall | 1837-45: Runcorn (Grappenhall); 1845-96: Warrington (Latchford); 1896-1974: Runcorn (Budworth, Stockton Heath); from 1974: Warrington. |
| Greasby | 1837-1974: Wirral (Woodchurch, West Wirral); from 1974: Birkenhead [Mers.]. |
| Great Boughton | 1837-69: Great Boughton (Chester Castle Division); 1870-1937: Chester (Great Boughton, Chester Castle, Chester Rural); 1937-74: West Cheshire (Chester Castle); from 1974: Chester & Ellesmere Port. |
| Great Budworth | 1837-1974: Runcorn (Budworth, Stockton Heath); from 1974: Vale Royal. |
| Great Meols | 1837-94: Wirral (Woodchurch); from 1894: see Hoylake cum West Kirby CP. |
| Great Mollington | 1837-69: Great Boughton (Chester Castle Division); 1870-1901: Chester (Great Boughton, Chester Castle); from 1901: see Mollington CP. |
| Great Neston | 1837-94: Wirral (Neston); from 1894: see Neston cum Parkgate CP. |
| Great Saughall | 1837-69: Great Boughton (Hawarden); 1870-1937: Chester (Hawarden, Chester Cathedral, Chester Rural); 1937-48: West Cheshire (Chester Castle); from 1948: see Saughall CP. |
| Great Stanney | 1837-69: Great Boughton (Chester Cathedral Division); 1870-1937: Chester (Great Boughton, Chester Cathedral, Chester Rural); 1937-1950: West Cheshire (Chester Castle); from 1950: see Ellesmere Port CP. |
| Great Sutton | 1837-1937: Wirral (Eastham); 1937-50: West Cheshire (Chester Castle); from 1950: see Ellesmere Port CP. |
| Great Warford | 1837-1974: Macclesfield (Alderley, Macclesfield, Macclesfield Rural); from 1974: Macclesfield |

| | |
|---|---|
| Guilden Sutton | 1837-69: Great Boughton (Chester Castle Division); 1870-1937: Chester (Tattenhall); 1937-74: West Cheshire (Chester Castle); from 1974: Chester & Ellesmere Port. |
| Hale | 1837-98: Altrincham (Altrincham); 1898-1974: Bucklow (Altrincham); from 1974: Trafford [*Gtr. Man.*]. |
| Halton | 1837-1967: Runcorn (Runcorn); from 1967: see Runcorn CP. |
| Hampton | 1837-53: Nantwich (Wrenbury); 1853-1937: Whitchurch (Whitchurch, Malpas); 1937-74: West Cheshire (Tarvin Rural); from 1974: Chester & Ellesmere Port. |
| Handforth | 1837-77: see Handforth cum Bosden CP; 1877-1936: Stockport (Cheadle); from 1936: see Wilmslow, Cheadle & Gatley CPs. |
| Handforth cum Bosden | 1837-77: Stockport (Cheadle, Hazel Grove); from 1877: see Bosden, Handforth CPs. |
| Handley | 1837-69: Great Boughton (Tattenhall); 1870-1937: Chester (Tattenhall); 1937-74: West Cheshire (Tarvin Rural); from 1974: Chester & Ellesmere Port. |
| Hankelow | 1837-1937: Nantwich (Wrenbury); 1937-74: Crewe (Nantwich); 1974-88: Congleton & Crewe; from 1988: South Cheshire. |
| Hapsford | 1837-69: Great Boughton (Chester Cathedral Division); 1870-1937: Chester (Great Boughton, Chester Cathedral, Chester Rural); 1937-1974: West Cheshire (Chester Castle); from 1974: Chester & Ellesmere Port. |
| Hartford | 1837-1974: Northwich (Weaverham, Northwich); from 1974: Northwich. |
| Harthill | 1837-69: Great Boughton (Tattenhall); 1870-1937: Chester (Tattenhall); 1937-74: West Cheshire (Tarvin Rural); from 1974: Chester & Ellesmere Port. |
| Haslington | 1837-1937: Nantwich (Wybunbury, Crewe, Haslington); 1937-74: Crewe (Crewe); 1974-88: Congleton & Crewe; from 1988: South Cheshire. |
| Hassall | 1837-1937: Congleton (Sandbach); 1937-74: Crewe (Sandbach); 1974-88: Congleton & Crewe; from 1988: South Cheshire. |
| Hatherton | 1837-1937: Nantwich (Wybunbury, Crewe, Nantwich); 1937-74: Crewe (Nantwich); 1974-88: Congleton & Crewe; from 1988: South Cheshire. |
| Hattersley | 1837-1936: Ashton-under-Lyne (Mottram); from 1936: see Hyde, Longendale CPs. |
| Hatton (nr. Runcorn) | 1837-1974: Runcorn (Grappenhall, Daresbury, Budworth, Stockton Heath); from 1974: Warrington. |

| | |
|---|---|
| Hatton (nr. Tattenhall) | 1837-69: Great Boughton (Tattenhall); 1870-1937: Chester (Tattenhall); 1937-74: West Cheshire (Tarvin Rural); from 1974: Chester & Ellesmere Port. |
| Haughton | 1837-1937: Nantwich (Bunbury, Wrenbury); 1937-74: Crewe (Nantwich); 1974-88: Congleton & Crewe; from 1988: South Cheshire. |
| Hazel Grove cum Bramhall | 1837-1900: see Bosden, Bramhall, Norbury, Offerton, Torkington CPs.; 1900-37: Stockport (Hazel Grove, Marple); 1937-74: North East Cheshire (Hazel Grove); from 1974: Stockport [*Gtr. Man.*]. |
| Heaton Norris | 1837-1913: in *Lancs.*; 1913-1936: Stockport (Heaton Norris); from 1936: see Stockport CP. |
| Helsby | 1837-1974: Runcorn (Frodsham, Runcorn); from 1974: Vale Royal. |
| Henbury | 1837-1936: see Henbury cum Pexall, Birtles, Macclesfield CPs; 1936-74: Macclesfield (Alderley, Gawsworth, Macclesfield, Macclesfield Rural); from 1974: Macclesfield. |
| Henbury cum Pexall | 1837-1936: Macclesfield (Alderley); fro 1936: see Henbury CP. |
| Henhull | 1837-1937: Nantwich (Nantwich); 1937-74: Crewe (Nantwich); 1974-88: Congleton & Crewe; from 1988: South Cheshire. |
| Heswall cum Oldfield | 1837-1974: Wirral (Neston, West Wirral); from 1974: Birkenhead [*Mers.*]. |
| Higher Bebington | 1837-1922: Wirral (Eastham, Bebington); from 1922: see Bebington cum Bromborough CP. |
| Higher Whitley | 1837-1936: Runcorn (Budworth); from 1936: see Whitley CP. |
| High Legh | 1837-98: Altrincham (Lymm); 1898-1974: Bucklow (Lymm, Knutsford, Lymm); from 1974: Macclesfield. |
| Hilbre Island | 1837-94: see Little Meols CP; from 1894: see Hoylake cum West Kirby CP. |
| Hockenhull | 1837-69: Great Boughton (Chester Castle Division); 1870-1937: Chester (Great Boughton, Tattenhall); 1937-74: West Cheshire (Tarvin Rural); from 1974: Chester & Ellesmere Port. |
| Hollingworth | 1837-1936: Ashton-under-Lyne (Mottram); from 1936: see Longendale CP. |
| Holmes Chapel | See Church Hulme CP. |
| Holy Trinity | 1837-69: Great Boughton (Chester Castle Division); 1870-84: Chester (Chester Cathedral); from 1884: see Chester CP. |

| | |
|---|---|
| Hoole | 1837-69: Great Boughton (Chester Cathedral Division); 1870-1937: Chester (Great Boughton, Chester Cathedral, Chester Rural); 1937-1954: West Cheshire (Chester Castle); from 1954: see Chester, Hoole Village, Guilden Sutton CPs. |
| Hoole Village: | 1837-94: see Hoole CP; 1894-1937: Chester (Chester Cathedral, Chester Rural); 1937-74: West Cheshire (Chester Castle); from 1974: Chester & Ellesmere Port. |
| Hoose | 1837-94: Wirral (Woodchurch); from 1894: see Hoylake cum West Kirby CP. |
| Hooton | 1837-1937: Wirral (Eastham); 1937-1974: West Cheshire (Chester Castle); from 1974: Chester & Ellesmere Port. |
| Horton | 1837-69: Great Boughton (Tattenhall); 1870-1937: Chester (Tattenhall); 1937-74: West Cheshire (Tarvin Rural); from 1974: Chester & Ellesmere Port. |
| Horton cum Peel | 1837-69: Great Boughton (Chester Castle Division); 1870-1937: Chester (Great Boughton, Tattenhall); 1937-74: West Cheshire (Tarvin Rural); from 1974: Chester & Ellesmere Port. |
| Hough | 1837-1937: Nantwich (Wybunbury, Crewe, Nantwich); 1937-74: Crewe (Nantwich); 1974-88: Congleton & Crewe; from 1988: South Cheshire. |
| Hoylake cum West Kirby | 1837-94: see West Kirby, Little Meols, Hoose, Great Meols, Grange CPs; 1894-1974: Wirral (Woodchurch, West Wirral); from 1974: Birkenhead [*Mers.*]. |
| Hulme | See Church Hulme, Kinderton cum Hulme CPs. |
| Hulme Walfield | 1837-1937: Congleton (Congleton); 1937-74: Macclesfield (Congleton); 1974-88: Congleton & Crewe; from 1988: South Cheshire. |
| Hulse | 1837-92: Northwich (Northwich); from 1892: see Lach Dennis CP. |
| Hunsterson | 1837-1937: Nantwich (Wybunbury, Crewe, Nantwich); 1937-74: Crewe (Nantwich); 1974-88: Congleton & Crewe; from 1988: South Cheshire. |
| Huntington | 1837-69: Great Boughton (Chester Castle Division); 1870-1937: Chester (Great Boughton, Tattenhall); 1937-74: West Cheshire (Chester Castle); from 1974: Chester & Ellesmere Port. |
| Hurdsfield | 1837-1974: Macclesfield (Bollington, Macclesfield, Macclesfield Rural); from 1974: Macclesfield. |
| Huxley | 1837-69: Great Boughton (Tattenhall); 1870-1937: Chester (Tattenhall); 1937-74: West Cheshire (Tarvin Rural); from 1974: Chester & Ellesmere Port. |

| | |
|---|---|
| Hyde | 1837-1937: Stockport (Hyde, Newton); 1937-74: Hyde (Hyde); from 1974: Tameside [*Gtr. Man.*]. |
| Iddinshall | 1837-69: Great Boughton (Tattenhall); 1870-1937: Chester (Tattenhall); 1937-74: West Cheshire (Tarvin Rural); from 1974: Chester & Ellesmere Port. |
| Ince | 1837-69: Great Boughton (Chester Cathedral Division); 1870-1937: Chester (Great Boughton, Chester Cathedral, Chester Rural); 1937-1950: West Cheshire (Chester Castle); from 1950: see Ellesmere Port CP. |
| Irby | 1837-1974: Wirral (Woodchurch, West Cheshire); from 1974: Birkenhead [*Mers.*]. |
| Keckwick | 1837-1936: Runcorn (Grappenhall, Daresbury, Budworth); from 1936: see Daresbury CP. |
| Kelsall | 1837-69: Great Boughton (Chester Castle Division); 1870-1937: Chester (Great Boughton, Tattenhall); 1937-74: West Cheshire (Tarvin Rural); from 1974: Chester & Ellesmere Port. |
| Kermincham | 1837-1936: Congleton (Church Hulme); from 1936: see Swettenham CP. |
| Kerridge | 1837-94: see Bollington CP; 1894-1900: Macclesfield (Bollington); from 1900: see Bollington CP. |
| Kettleshulme | 1837-1974: Macclesfield (Rainow, Bollington, Macclesfield, Macclesfield Rural); from 1974: Macclesfield. |
| Kinderton | 1837-94: see Kinderton cum Hulme, Newton CPs; 1894-1936: Northwich (Middlewich); from 1936: see Sproston, Muddlewich, Bradwall CPs. |
| Kinderton cum Hulme | 1837-94: Northwich (Middlewich); from 1894: see Middlewich, Kinderton CPs. |
| Kingsley | 1837-1974: Runcorn (Frodsham, Runcorn); from 1974: Vale Royal. |
| King's Marsh | 1837-69: Great Boughton (Tattenhall); 1870-1937: Chester (Tattenhall); 1937-74: West Cheshire (Tarvin Rural); from 1974: Chester & Ellesmere Port. |
| Kingswood | 1837-1936: Runcorn (Frodsham); from 1936: see Manley, Kingsley, Norley CPs. |
| Kinnerton | See Lower Kinnerton CP. |
| Knutsford | 1837-95: see Knutsford Inferior, Knutsford Superior CPs; 1895-98: Altrincham (Knutsford); 1898-1974: Bucklow (Knutsford); from 1974: Macclesfield. |
| Knutsford Inferior | 1837-95: Altrincham (Knutsford); from 1895: see Knutsford CP. |
| Knutsford Superior | 1837-95: Altrincham (Knutsford); from 1895: see Knutsford CP. |

| | |
|---|---|
| Lach Dennis | 1837-1974: Northwich (Middlewich, Northwich); from 1974: Vale Royal. |
| Landican | 1837-1933: Wirral (Woodchurch); from 1933: see Birkenhead CP. |
| Larkton | 1837-53: Nantwich (Wrenbury); 1853-1937: Whitchurch (Whitchurch, Malpas); 1937-74: West Cheshire (Tarvin Rural); from 1974: Chester & Ellesmere Port. |
| Latchford | 1837-45: Runcorn (Grappenhall); 1845-96: Warrington (Latchford); 1896: Runcorn (Budworth) [1896-1937 (pt of Warrington CP from 1933): Warrington; 1937-74: Newton; from 1974: Warrington] |
| Latchford Without | 1837-94: see Latchford CP; 1894-96: Warrington (Latchford); 1896-1936: Runcorn (Budworth); from 1936: see Stockton Heath CP. |
| Lawton | See Church Lawton CP. |
| Lea (nr. Crewe) | 1837-1937: Nantwich (Wybunbury, Crewe, Nantwich); 1937-74: Crewe (Nantwich); 1974-88: Congleton & Crewe; from 1988: South Cheshire. |
| Lea by Backford | 1837-69: Great Boughton (Chester Cathedral Division); 1870-1937: Chester (Great Boughton, Chester Cathedral, Chester Rural); 1937-1974: West Cheshire (Chester Castle); from 1974: Chester & Ellesmere Port. |
| Lea Newbold | 1837-69: Great Boughton (Tattenhall); 1870-1937: Chester (Tattenhall); 1937-74: West Cheshire (Chester Castle); from 1974: Chester & Ellesmere Port. |
| Ledsham | 1837-1937: Wirral (Neston, Eastham); 1937-74: West Cheshire (Chester Castle); from 1974: Chester & Ellesmere Port. |
| Leese | 1837-1936: Congleton (Church Hulme); from 1936: see Cranage, Lach Dennis, Byley CPs. |
| Leftwich | 1837-1936: Northwich (Northwich); from 1936: see Davenham, Northwich CPs). |
| Leigh | See High Legh, Little Leigh CPs. |
| Leighton (nr. Nantwich) | 1837-1937: Nantwich (Nantwich, Crewe, Haslington); 1937-74: Crewe (Crewe); 1974-88: Congleton & Crewe; from 1988: South Cheshire. |
| Leighton (nr. Neston) | 1837-94: Wirral (Neston); from 1974: see Neston cum Parkgate CP. |
| Liscard | 1837-61: Wirral (Wallasey); 1861-1912: Birkenhead (Wallasey); from 1912: see Wallasey CP. |
| Little Budworth | 1837-1974: Northwich (Over, Winsford); from 1974: Vale Royal. |

| | |
|---|---|
| Little Leigh | 1837-1974: Northwich (Weaverham, Northwich); from 1974: Vale Royal. |
| Little Meols | 1837-94: Wirral (Woodchurch); from 1894: see Hoylake cum West Kirby CP. |
| Little Mollington | 1837-69: Great Boughton (Chester Castle Division); 1870-1901: Chester (Great Boughton, Chester Castle); from 1901: see Mollington CP. |
| Little Neston | 1837-94: Wirral (Neston); from 1894: see Neston cum Parkgate CP. |
| Little Saughall | 1837-69: Great Boughton (Hawarden); 1870-1937: Chester (Hawarden, Chester Cathedral, Chester Rural); 1937-48: West Cheshire (Chester Castle); from 1948: see Saughall CP. |
| Little Stanney | 1837-69: Great Boughton (Chester Cathedral Division); 1870-1937: Chester (Great Boughton, Chester Cathedral, Chester Rural); 1937-1974: West Cheshire (Chester Castle); from 1974: Chester & Ellesmere Port. |
| Little Sutton | 1837-1937: Wirral (Eastham); 1937-50: West Cheshire (Chester Castle); from 1950: see Ellesmere Port CP. |
| Littleton | 1837-69: Great Boughton (Chester Castle Division); 1870-1937: Chester (Great Boughton, Chester Castle, Chester Rural); 1937-74: West Cheshire (Chester Castle); from 1974: Chester & Ellesmere Port. |
| Little Warford | 1837-1951: see Marthall cum Warford CP; 1951-74: Bucklow (Knutsford); from 1974: Macclesfield. |
| Longendale | 1837-1936: see Mottram, Hollingworth, Matley, Hattersley CPs; 1936-37: Ashton-under-Lyne (Mottram, Stalybridge); 1937-74: Hyde (Stalybridge, Dukinfield & Stalybridge CP); from 1974: Tameside [Gtr. Man.]. |
| Lostock Gralam | 1837-1974: Northwich (Northwich); from 1974: Vale Royal. |
| Lower Bebington | 1837-1922: Wirral (Eastham, Bebington); from 1922: see Bebington cum Bromborough CP. |
| Lower Kinnerton | 1837-69: Great Boughton (Hawarden); 1870-1937: Chester (Hawarden, Chester Castle, Chester Rural); 1937-74: West Cheshire (Chester Castle); from 1974: Chester & Ellesmere Port. |
| Lower Peover | See Peover Inferior CP. |
| Lower Whitley | 1837-1936: Runcorn (Budworth); from 1936: see Whitley CP. |
| Lower Withington | 1837-1936: Macclesfield (Alderley); from 1936: see Withington CP. |
| Lyme Handley | 1837-1974: Macclesfield (Bollington, Macclesfield, Macclesfield Rural); from 1974: Macclesfield. |

| | |
|---|---|
| Lymm | 1837-98: Altrincham (Lymm); 1898-1974: Bucklow (Lymm, Knutsford, Lymm); from 1974: Warrington. |
| Macclesfield | 1837-1974: Macclesfield (East Macclesfield, West Macclesfield, Sutton, Macclesfield, Macclesfield & Bollington); from 1974: Macclesfield. |
| Macclesfield Forest | 1837-1974: Macclesfield (Rainow, Gawsworth, Macclesfield, Macclesfield & Bollington); from 1974: Macclesfield. |
| Macefen | 1837-53: Nantwich (Wrenbury); 1853-1937: Whitchurch (Whitchurch, Malpas); 1937-74: West Cheshire (Tarvin Rural); from 1974: Chester & Ellesmere Port. |
| Malpas | 1837-53: Wrexham (Malpas); 1853-1937: Whitchurch (Whitchurch, Malpas); 1937-74: West Cheshire (Tarvin Rural); from 1974: Chester & Ellesmere Port. |
| Manley | 1837-1974: Runcorn (Frodsham, Runcorn); from 1974: Vale Royal. |
| Marbury (nr. Northwich) | 1837-1974: Northwich (Northwich); from 1974: Vale Royal. |
| Marbury cum Quoisley | 1837-53: Nantwich (Wrenbury); 1853-1937: Whitchurch (Whitchurch); 1937-74: Crewe (Nantwich); 1974-88: Congleton & Crewe; from 1988: South Cheshire. |
| Marlston cum Lache | 1837-1936: Macclesfield (Alderley); from 1936: see Withington CP. |
| Marple | 1837-1937: Stockport (Marple, Hazel Grove, Marple); 1936-37: Glossop (Glossop); 1936-37: Hayfield (Hayfield); 1937-74: North East Cheshire (Hazel Grove); from 1974: Stockport [*Gtr. Man.*]. |
| Marston | 1837-1974: Northwich (Northwich); from 1974: Vale Royal. |
| Marthall | 1837-1951: see Marthall cum Warford; 1951-74: Bucklow (Knutsford); from 1974: Macclesfield. |
| Marthall cum Warford | 1837-98: Altrincham (Knutsford); 1898-1951: Bucklow (Knutsford); from 1951: see Marthall. |
| Marton (nr. Congleton) | 1837-1974: Macclesfield (Gawsworth, Macclesfield, Macclesfield Rural); from 1974: Macclesfield. |
| Marton (nr. Winsford) | 1837-1974: Northwich (Over, Winsford); from 1974: Vale Royal. |
| Matley | 1837-1936: Ashton-under-Lyne (Stayley, Dukinfield, Stalybridge); from 1936: see Stalybridge, Hyde, Dukinfield, Longendale CPs). |
| Meols | See Great Meols, Little Meols CPs. |
| Mere | 1837-98: Altrincham (Knutsford); 1898-1974: Bucklow (Knutsford); from 1974: Macclesfield. |

| | |
|---|---|
| Mickle Trafford | 1837-69: Great Boughton (Chester Cathedral Division); 1870-1937: Chester (Great Boughton, Chester Cathedral, Chester Rural); 1937-1974: West Cheshire (Chester Castle); from 1974: Chester & Ellesmere Port. |
| Middlewich | 1837-1974: Northwich (Middlewich, Winsford); 1974-88: Congleton & Crewe; from 1988: South Cheshire. |
| Millington | 1837-98: Altrincham (Knutsford); 1898-1974: Bucklow (Knutsford); from 1974: Macclesfield. |
| Minshull | See Church Minshull, Minshull Vernon CPs. |
| Minshull Vernon | 1837-1937: Nantwich (Nantwich, Crewe, Haslington); 1937-74: Crewe (Crewe); 1974-88: Congleton & Crewe; from 1988: South Cheshire. |
| Mobberley | 1837-98: Altrincham (Wilmslow); 1898-1974: Bucklow (Wilmslow, Knutsford); from 1974: Macclesfield. |
| Mollington | 1837-1901: see Great Mollington, Little Mollington CPs; 1901-37: Chester (Chester Cathedral, Chester Rural); 1937-74: West Cheshire (Chester Castle); from 1974: Chester & Ellesmere Port. |
| Monks Coppenhall | 1837-1937: Nantwich (Wybunbury, Crewe, Crewe Borough); 1937-74: Crewe (Crewe); 1974-88: Congleton & Crewe; from 1988: South Cheshire. |
| Moore | 1837-1974: Runcorn (Grappenhall, Daresbury, Budworth, Stockton Heath); from 1974: Halton. |
| Mooresbarrow with Parme | 1837-92: Northwich (Middlewich); from 1892: see Sproston CP. |
| Moreton (nr. Wallasey) | 1837-1928: Wirral (Woodchurch); from 1928: see Wallasey CP. |
| Moreton cum Alcumlow | 1837-1937: Congleton (Congleton); 1937-74: Crewe (Sandbach); 1974-88: Congleton & Crewe; from 1988: South Cheshire. |
| Moston (nr. Chester) | 1837-69: Great Boughton (Chester Cathedral Division); 1870-1937: Chester (Great Boughton, Chester Cathedral, Chester Rural); 1937-1974: West Cheshire (Chester Castle); from 1974: Chester & Ellesmere Port. |
| Moston (nr. Sandbach) | 1837-1936: Congleton (Sandbach); 1936-70: see Tetton CP; 1970-74: Crewe (Sandbach); 1974-88: Congleton & Crewe; from 1988: South Cheshire. |
| Mottram | 1837-1936: Ashton-under-Lyne (Mottram); from 1936: see Longendale CP. |
| Mottram St. Andrew | 1837-1974: Macclesfield (Prestbury, Macclesfield, Macclesfield Rural); from 1974: Macclesfield. |

| | |
|---|---|
| Mouldsworth | 1837-69: Great Boughton (Chester Castle Division); 1870-1937: Chester (Great Boughton, Tattenhall); 1937-74: West Cheshire (Tarvin Rural); from 1974: Chester & Ellesmere Port |
| Moulton | 1837-1974: Northwich (Over, Winsford); from 1974: Vale Royal. |
| Nantwich | 1837-1937: Nantwich (Nantwich); 1937-74: Crewe (Nantwich); 1974-88: Congleton & Crewe; from 1988: South Cheshire. |
| Ness | 1837-1974: Wirral (Neston, Ness); from 1974: Chester & Ellesmere Port. |
| Neston cum Parkgate | 1837-94: see Great Neston, Little Neston, Leighton CPs; 1894-1974: Wirral (Neston, West Wirral); from 1974: Chester & Ellesmere Port. |
| Nether Alderley | 1837-1974: Macclesfield (Alderley, Macclesfield, Macclesfield Rural); from 1974: Macclesfield. |
| Nether Peover | 1837-1974: Northwich (Northwich); from 1974: Vale Royal. |
| Netherpool | 1837-1911: Wirral (Eastham); from 1911: see Ellesmere Port CP. |
| Newbold Astbury | 1837-1937: Congleton (Congleton); 1937-74: Macclesfield (Congleton); 1974-88: Congleton & Crewe; from 1988: South Cheshire. |
| Newhall (nr. Audlem) | 1837-1937: Nantwich (Wrenbury); 1937-74: Crewe (Nantwich); 1974-88: Congleton & Crewe; from 1988: South Cheshire. |
| Newhall (nr. Middlewich) | 1837-92: Northwich (Middlewich); from 1892: see Lach Dennis CP. |
| Newton (nr. Hyde) | 1837-1923: Ashton-under-Lyne (Newton); from 1923: see Hyde CP. |
| Newton (nr. Middlewich) | 1837-94: Northwich (Middlewich); from 1894: see Middlewich, Kinderton CPs. |
| Newton (nr. Prestbury) | 1837-1936: Macclesfield (Prestbury); from 1936: see Mottram St. Andrew CP. |
| Newton by Chester | 1837-69: Great Boughton (Chester Cathedral Division); 1870-1936: Chester (Great Boughton, Chester Cathedral, Chester Rural); from 1936: see Chester, Hoole CPs. |
| Newton by Daresbury | 1837-1936: Runcorn (Grappenhall, Daresbury, Budworth); from 1936: see Daresbury CP. |
| Newton by Frodsham | 1837-1936: Runcorn (Frodsham); from 1936: see Kingsley CP. |
| Newton by Malpas | 1837-53: Wrexham (Malpas); 1853-1937: Whitchurch (Whitchurch, Malpas); 1937-74: West Cheshire (Tarvin Rural); from 1974: Chester & Ellesmere Port. |

| | |
|---|---|
| Newton by Tattenhall | 1837-69: Great Boughton (Tattenhall); 1870-1937: Chester (Tattenhall); 1936-74: West Cheshire (Tarvin Rural); from 1974: Chester & Ellesmere Port. |
| Newton cum Larton | 1837-1888: Wirral (Woodchurch); from 1888: see Grange CP. |
| Noctorum | 1837-61: Wirral (Woodchurch); 1861-1933: Birkenhead (Tranmere); from 1933: see Birkenhead CP. |
| Norbury (nr. Malpas) | 1837-53: Nantwich (Wrenbury); 1853-1937: Whitchurch (Whitchurch); 1937-74: Crewe (Nantwich); 1974-88: Congleton & Crewe; from 1988: South Cheshire. |
| Norbury (nr. Stockport) | 1837-1900: Stockport (Hazel Grove); from 1900: see Hazel Grove cum Bramhall CP. |
| Norley | 1837-1974: Runcorn (Frodsham, Runcorn); from 1974: Vale Royal. |
| Northenden | 1837-98: Altrincham (Wilmslow); 1898-1931: Bucklow (Wilmslow); from 1931: see Manchester CP [*Lancs.*]. |
| Northen Etchells | 1837-98: Altrincham (Wilmslow); 1898-1931: Bucklow (Wilmslow); from 1931: see Manchester CP [*Lancs.*]. |
| North Rode | 1837-1974: Macclesfield (Gawsworth, Macclesfield, Macclesfield Rural); from 1974: Macclesfield. |
| Northwich | 1837-1974: Northwich (Northwich, Weaverham); from 1974: Vale Royal. |
| Norton | 1837-1967: Runcorn (Runcorn); from 1967: see Runcorn CP. |
| Oakmere | 1837-1974: Northwich (Weaverham, Winsford); from 1974: Vale Royal. |
| Occlestone | 1837-92: Northwich (Middlewich); from 1892: see Wimboldsley CP. |
| Odd Rode | 1837-1937: Congleton (Sandbach); 1937-74: Crewe (Sandbach); 1974-88: Congleton & Crewe; from 1988: South Cheshire. |
| Offerton | 1837-1900: Stockport (Marple); from 1900: see Hazel Grove cum Bramhall CP. |
| Oldcastle | 1837-53: Wrexham (Malpas); 1853-1937: Whitchurch (Whitchurch, Malpas); 1937-74: West Cheshire (Tarvin Rural); from 1974: Chester & Ellesmere Port. |
| Old Withington | 1837-1936: Macclesfield (Alderley); from 1936: see Withington CP. |
| Ollerton | 1837-98: Altrincham (Knutsford); 1898-1974: Bucklow (Knutsford); from 1974: Macclesfield. |
| Onston | 1837-92: Northwich (Weaverham); from 1892: see Crowton CP. |

| | |
|---|---|
| Oulton Lowe | 1837-92: Northwich (Over); from 1892: see Little Budworth CP. |
| Over | 1837-1936: Northwich (Over); from 1936: see Winsford, Darnhall, Marton CPs. |
| Over Alderley | 1837-1974: Macclesfield (Alderley, Macclesfield, Macclesfield Rural); from 1974: Macclesfield. |
| Over Peover | See Peover Superior CP. |
| Overpool | 1837-1911: Wirral (Eastham); from 1911: see Ellesmere Port CP. |
| Overton | 1837-53: Wrexham (Malpas); 1853-1937: Whitchurch (Whitchurch, Malpas); 1937-74: West Cheshire (Tarvin Rural); from 1974: Chester & Ellesmere Port. |
| Oxton | 1837-61: Wirral (Woodchurch); 1861-1933: Birkenhead (Tranmere); from 1933: see Birkenhead CP. |
| Parkgate | See Neston cum Parkgate CP. |
| Partington | 1837-98: Altrincham (Lymm); 1898-1974: Bucklow (Lymm, Knutsford, Lymm); from 1974: Trafford. |
| Peckforton | 1837-1937: Nantwich (Bunbury, Wrenbury); 1937-74: Crewe (Nantwich); 1974-88: Congleton & Crewe; from 1988: South Cheshire. |
| Pensby | 1837-1974: Wirral (Woodchurch, West Wirral); from 1974: Birkenhead [Mers.]. |
| Peover | See Nether Peover, Peover Inferior, Peover Superior CPs. |
| Peover Inferior | 1837-98: Altrincham (Knutsford); 1898-1974: Bucklow (Knutsford); from 1974: Macclesfield. |
| Peover Superior | 1837-98: Altrincham (Knutsford); 1898-1974: Bucklow (Knutsford); from 1974: Macclesfield. |
| Pickmere | 1837-98: Altrincham (Knutsford); 1898-1974: Bucklow (Knutsford); from 1974: Macclesfield. |
| Picton | 1837-69: Great Boughton (Chester Cathedral Division); 1870-1937: Chester (Great Boughton, Chester Cathedral, Chester Rural); 1937-1974: West Cheshire (Chester Castle); from 1974: Chester & Ellesmere Port. |
| Plumley | 1837-98: Altrincham (Knutsford); 1898-1974: Bucklow (Knutsford); from 1974: Macclesfield. |
| Poole | 1837-1937: Nantwich (Nantwich); 1937-74: Crewe (Nantwich); 1974-88: Congleton & Crewe; from 1988: South Cheshire. |
| Pott Shrigley | 1837-1974: Macclesfield (Bollington, Macclesfield, Macclesfield Rural); from 1974: Macclesfield. |
| Poulton (nr. Chester) | 1837-69: Great Boughton (Hawarden); 1870-1937: Chester (Hawarden, Chester Castle, Chester Rural); 1937-74: West Cheshire (Chester Castle); from 1974: Chester & Ellesmere Port. |

| | |
|---|---|
| Poulton cum Seacombe | 1837-61: Wirral (Wallasey); 1861-1912: Birkenhead (Wallasey); from 1912: see Wallasey CP. |
| Poulton cum Spital | 1837-1974: Wirral (Eastham, Bromborough, East Wirral, Clatterbridge); from 1974: Birkenhead [*Mers.*] |
| Pownall Fee | 1837-94: Altrincham (Wilmslow); from 1894: see Wilmslow, Styal CPs. |
| Poynton | 1837-80: Macclesfield (Prestbury); from 1880: see Poynton with Worth CP. |
| Poynton with Worth | 1837-80: see Poynton,Worth CPs; 1880-1974: Macclesfield (Prestbury, Macclesfield, Macclesfield Rural); from 1974: Macclesfield. |
| Prenton | 1837-1933: Wirral (Woodchurch); from 1933: see Birkenhead CP. |
| Prestbury | 1837-1974: Macclesfield (Prestbury, Macclesfield, Macclesfield Rural); from 1974: Macclesfield. |
| Preston Brook | 1837-1936: see Preston on the Hill, Norton CPs; 1936-74: Runcorn (Budworth, Stockton Heath); from 1974: Halton. |
| Preston on the Hill | 1837-1936: Runcorn (Grappenhall, Daresbury, Budworth); from 1936: see Preston Brook CP. |
| Prior's Heys | 1837-69: Great Boughton (Chester Castle Division); 1870-1937: Chester (Great Boughton, Tattenhall); 1937-74: West Cheshire (Tarvin Rural); from 1974: Chester & Ellesmere Port. |
| Puddington | 1837-1937: Wirral (Neston, Eastham); 1937-74: West Cheshire (Chester Castle); from 1974: Chester & Ellesmere Port. |
| Pulford | 1837-69: Great Boughton (Hawarden); 1870-1937: Chester (Hawarden, Chester Castle, Chester Rural); 1937-74: West Cheshire (Chester Castle); from 1974: Chester & Ellesmere Port. |
| Raby | 1837-1974: Wirral (Neston, Ness); from 1974: Chester & Ellesmere Port. |
| Radnor | 1837-95: Congleton (Congleton); from 1895: see Somerford Booths CP. |
| Rainow | 1837-1974: Macclesfield (Rainow, Bollington, Macclesfield, Macclesfield Rural); from 1974: Chester & Ellesmere Port. |
| Ravenscroft | 1837-92: Northwich (Middlewich); from 1892: see Byley CP. |
| Reddish | 1837-1901: *in Lancs.*; 1901-36: Stockport (Heaton Norris, Stockport Third); from 1936: see Stockport CP. |

| | |
|---|---|
| Ridley | 1837-1937: Nantwich (Bunbury, Wrenbury); 1937-74: Crewe (Nantwich); 1974-88: Congleton & Crewe; from 1988: South Cheshire. |
| Ringway | 1837-1900: see Hale CP; 1900-74: Bucklow (Altrincham); from 1974: Trafford [*Gtr. Man.*]. |
| Rock Ferry | 1837-94: see Higher Bebington CP; 1894-98: Wirral (Bebington); from 1898: see Birkenhead CP. |
| Rode | See North Rode, Odd Rode CPs. |
| Romiley | 1837-1936: Stockport (Marple, Bredbury); from 1936: see Bredbury & Romiley CP. |
| Rope | 1837-1937: Nantwich (Wybunbury, Crewe, Nantwich); 1937-74: Crewe (Nantwich); 1974-88: Congleton & Crewe; from 1988: South Cheshire. |
| Rostherne | 1837-98: Altrincham (Knutsford); 1898-1974: Bucklow (Knutsford); from 1974: Macclesfield. |
| Rowton | 1837-69: Great Boughton (Chester Castle Division); 1870-1937: Chester (Great Boughton, Tattenhall); 1937-74: West Cheshire (Chester Castle); from 1974: Chester & Ellesmere Port. |
| Rudheath | 1837-1974: Northwich (Middlewich, Northwich); from 1974: Vale Royal. |
| Runcorn | 1837-1974: Runcorn (Runcorn); from 1974: Halton. |
| Rushton | 1837-1892: Nantwich (Bunbury); 1892-1937: Chester (Tattenhall); 1937-74: Northwich (Winsford); from 1974: Vale Royal. |
| Saighton | 1837-69: Great Boughton (Tattenhall); 1870-1937: Chester (Tattenhall); 1937-74: West Cheshire (Chester Castle); from 1974: Chester & Ellesmere Port. |
| St. Bridget | 1837-69: Great Boughton (Chester Cathedral Division); 1870-84: Chester (Chester Cathedral); from 1884: see Chester CP. |
| St. John the Baptist | 1837-69: Great Boughton (Chester Castle Division); 1870-84: Chester (Chester Castle); from 1884: see Chester CP. |
| St. Martin | 1837-69: Great Boughton (Chester Cathedral Division); 1870-84: Chester (Chester Cathedral); from 1884: see Chester CP. |
| St. Mary on the Hill | 1837-69: Great Boughton (Chester Castle Division); 1870-84: Chester (Chester Castle); from 1884: see Chester CP. |
| St. Michael | 1837-69: Great Boughton (Chester Castle Division); 1870-84: Chester (Chester Castle); from 1884: see Chester CP. |
| St. Olave | 1837-69: Great Boughton (Chester Castle Division); 1870-84: Chester (Chester Castle); from 1884: see Chester CP. |

| | |
|---|---|
| St. Oswald | 1837-69: Great Boughton (Chester Cathedral Division); 1870-84: Chester (Chester Cathedral); from 1884: see Chester CP. |
| St. Peter | 1837-69: Great Boughton (Chester Cathedral Division); 1870-84: Chester (Chester Cathedral); from 1884: see Chester CP. |
| Sale | 1837-98: Altrincham (Altrincham); 1898-1974: Bucklow (Altrincham, Sale); from 1974: Trafford [*Gtr. Man.*]. |
| Sandbach | 1837-1937: Congleton (Sandbach); 1937-74: Crewe (Sandbach); 1974-88: Congleton & Crewe; from 1988: South Cheshire. |
| Saughall | 1837-1948: see Great Saughall, Little Saughall CPs; 1948-74: West Cheshire (Chester Castle); from 1974: Chester & Ellesmere Port. |
| Saughall Massie | 1837-1933: Wirral (Woodchurch); from 1933: see Wallasey, Grange CPs. |
| Seven Oaks | 1837-1936: Runcorn (Budworth); from 1936: see Antrobus CP. |
| Shavington cum Gresty | 1837-1937: Nantwich (Wybunbury, Crewe, Haslington); 1937-74: Crewe (Crewe); 1974-88: Congleton & Crewe; from 1988: South Cheshire. |
| Shipbrook | 1837-92: Northwich (Middlewich); from 1892: see Whatcroft CP. |
| Shocklach | See Church Shocklach, Shocklach Oviatt CPs. |
| Shocklach Oviatt | 1837-97: Wrexham (Malpas, Holt); 1897-1937: Chester (Tattenhall); 1937-74: West Cheshire (Tarvin Rural); from 1974: Chester & Ellesmere Port. |
| Shotwick | 1837-69: Great Boughton (Hawarden); 1870-1937: Chester (Hawarden, Chester Castle, Chester Rural); 1937-74: West Cheshire (Chester Castle); from 1974: Chester & Ellesmere Port. |
| Shotwick Park | 1837-69: Great Boughton (Hawarden); 1870-1937: Chester (Hawarden, Chester Castle, Chester Rural); 1937-74: West Cheshire (Chester Castle); from 1974: Chester & Ellesmere Port. |
| Shurlach | 1837-92: Northwich (Northwich); from 1892: see Rudheath CP. |
| Siddington | 1837-1974: Macclesfield (Gawsworth, Macclesfield, Macclesfield Rural); from 1974: Macclesfield. |
| Smallwood | 1837-1937: Congleton (Sandbach); 1937-74: Crewe (Sandbach); 1974-88: Congleton & Crewe; from 1988: South Cheshire. |

| | |
|---|---|
| Snelson | 1837-1974: Macclesfield (Alderley, Macclesfield, Macclesfield Rural); from 1974: Macclesfield. |
| Somerford | 1837-1937: Congleton (Congleton); 1937-74: Macclesfield (Congleton); 1974-88: Congleton & Crewe; from 1988: South Cheshire. |
| Somerford Booths | 1837-1937: Congleton (Congleton); 1937-74: Macclesfield (Congleton); 1974-88: Congleton & Crewe; from 1988: South Cheshire. |
| Sound | 1837-1937: Nantwich (Wrenbury); 1937-74: Crewe (Nantwich); 1974-88: Congleton & Crewe; from 1988: South Cheshire. |
| Spital Boughton | 1837-69: Great Boughton (Chester Castle Division); 1870-84: Chester (Chester Castle); from 1884: see Chester CP. |
| Sproston | 1837-1974: Northwich (Middlewich, Winsford); from 1974: Vale Royal. |
| Spurstow | 1837-1937: Nantwich (Bunbury, Wrenbury); 1937-74: Crewe (Nantwich); 1974-88: Congleton & Crewe; from 1988: South Cheshire. |
| Stalybridge | 1837-94: see Stayley, Dukinfield CPs; 1894-1937: Ashton-under-Lyne (Dukinfield, Stalybridge); 1937-74: Hyde (Stalybridge, Dukinfield & Stalybridge); from 1974: Tameside [*Gtr. Man.*]. |
| Stanlow | 1837-69: Great Boughton (Chester Cathedral Division); 1870-1911: Chester (Great Boughton, Chester Cathedral), from 1911: see Great Stanney CP. |
| Stanney | See Great Stanney, Little Stanney CPs. |
| Stanthorne | 1837-1974: Northwich (Middlewich, Winsford); from 1974: Vale Royal. |
| Stapleford | See Bruen Stapleford, Foulk Stapleford CPs. |
| Stapeley | 1837-1937: Nantwich (Wybunbury, Crewe, Nantwich); 1937-74: Crewe (Nantwich); 1974-88: Congleton & Crewe; from 1988: South Cheshire. |
| Stayley | 1837-94: Ashton-under-Lyne (Stayley, Dukinfield); from 1894: see Stalybridge CP. |
| Stockham | 1837-1936: Runcorn (Runcorn); from 1936: see Norton CP. |
| Stockport | 1837-1974: Stockport (Stockport First, Stockport Second, Stockport Third); from 1974: Stockport [*Gtr. Man.*]. |
| Stockport Etchells | 1837-1930: Stockport (Cheadle); from 1930: see Cheadle & Gatley CP. |
| Stockton | 1837-53: Wrexham (Malpas); 1853-1937: Whitchurch (Whitchurch, Malpas); 1937-74: West Cheshire (Tarvin Rural); from 1974: Chester & Ellesmere Port. |

| | |
|---|---|
| Stockton Heath | 1837-97: see Appleton CP; 1897-1974: Runcorn (Budworth, Stockton Heath); from 1974: Warrington. |
| Stoke (nr. Chester) | 1837-69: Great Boughton (Chester Cathedral Division); 1870-1937: Chester (Great Boughton, Chester Cathedral, Chester Rural); 1937-1974: West Cheshire (Chester Castle); from 1974: Chester & Ellesmere Port. |
| Stoke (nr. Nantwich) | 1837-1937: Nantwich (Nantwich); 1937-74: Crewe (Nantwich); 1974-88: Congleton & Crewe; from 1988: South Cheshire. |
| Storeton | 1837-1974: Wirral (Eastham, Bebington, East Wirral); from 1974: Birkenhead [Mers.]. |
| Stretton (nr. Malpas) | 1837-69: Great Boughton (Tattenhall); 1870-1937: Chester (Tattenhall); 1937-74: West Cheshire (Tarvin Rural); from 1974: Chester & Ellesmere Port. |
| Stretton (nr. Runcorn) | 1837-1974: Runcorn (Budworth, Stockton Heath); from 1974: see Warrington. |
| Stublach | 1837-92: Northwich (Middlewich); from 1892: see Lach Dennis CP. |
| Styal | 1837-94: see Pownall Fee CP; 1894-98: Altrincham (Wilmslow); 1898-1936: Bucklow (Wilmslow); from 1936: see Wilmslow CP. |
| Sutton (nr. Macclesfield) | 1837-1974: Macclesfield (Sutton, Macclesfield, Macclesfield Rural); from 1974: Macclesfield. |
| Sutton (nr. Middlewich) | 1837-92: Northwich (Middlewich); from 1892: see Newton CP. |
| Sutton (nr. Runcorn) | 1837-1974: Runcorn (Runcorn); from 1974: Vale Royal. |
| Sutton | See also Great Sutton, Guilden Sutton, Little Sutton CPs. |
| Swettenham | 1837-1937: Congleton (Church Hulme); 1937-74: Crewe (Sandbach); 1974-88: Congleton & Crewe; from 1988: South Cheshire. |
| Tabley Inferior | 1837-94: Altrincham (Knutsford); 1894-1974: Bucklow (Knutsford); from 1974: Macclesfield. |
| Tabley Superior | 1837-94: Altrincham (Knutsford); 1894-1974: Bucklow (Knutsford); from 1974: Macclesfield. |
| Tarporley | 1837-1892: Nantwich (Bunbury); 1892-1937: Chester (Tattenhall); 1937-74: Northwich (Winsford); from 1974: Vale Royal. |
| Tarvin | 1837-69: Great Boughton (Chester Castle Division); 1870-1937: Chester (Great Boughton, Chester Castle, Chester Rural); 1937-74: West Cheshire (Tarvin Rural); from 1974: Chester & Ellesmere Port. |

| | |
|---|---|
| Tattenhall | 1837-69: Great Boughton (Tattenhall); 1870-1937: Chester (Tattenhall); 1937-74: West Cheshire (Tarvin Rural); from 1974: Chester & Ellesmere Port. |
| Tatton | 1837-94: Altrincham (Knutsford); 1894-1974: Bucklow (Knutsford); from 1974: Macclesfield. |
| Taxal | 1837-1936: Macclesfield (Rainow, Bollington); from 1936: see Hartington Upper Quarter [*Derb.*], Whaley Bridge [*Derb.*] and Wildboarclough CPs. |
| Tetton | 1837-1937: Congleton (Sandbach); 1937-70: Crewe (Sandbach); from 1970: see Moston CP. |
| Thelwall | 1837-45: Runcorn (Grappenhall); 1845-96: Warrington (Latchford); 1896-1936: Runcorn (Budworth); from 1936: see Grappenhall CP. |
| Thingwall | 1837-1933: Wirral (Woodchurch); from 1933: see Birkenhead CP. |
| Thornton Hough | 1837-1974: Wirral (Neston, East Wirral); from 1974: Birkenhead [*Mers.*]. |
| Thornton-le-Moors | 1837-69: Great Boughton (Chester Cathedral Division); 1870-1937: Chester (Great Boughton, Chester Cathedral, Chester Rural); 1937-1974: West Cheshire (Chester Castle); from 1974: Chester & Ellesmere Port. |
| Threapwood | 1837-96: Wrexham (Malpas, Holt); 1896-1937: Chester (Malpas); 1937-74: West Cheshire (Tarvin Rural); from 1974: Chester & Ellesmere Port. |
| Thurstaston | 1837-1974: Wirral (Woodchurch, West Wirral); from 1974: Birkenhead [*Mers.*] |
| Tilston | 1837-69: Great Boughton (Tattenhall); 1870-1937: Chester (Tattenhall); 1937-74: West Cheshire (Tarvin Rural); from 1974: Chester & Ellesmere Port. |
| Tilstone Fearnall | 1837-92: Nantwich (Bunbury); 1892-1937: Chester (Tattenhall); 1937-74: West Cheshire (Tarvin Rural); from 1974: Chester & Ellesmere Port. |
| Timperley | 1837-98: Altrincham (Altrincham); 1898-1936: Bucklow (Altrincham); from 1936: see Altrincham, Hale CPs. |
| Tintwistle | 1837-1937: Ashton-under-Lyne (Stayley, Mottram); 1937-74: Hyde (Stalybridge, Dukinfield & Stalybridge); from 1974: High Peak [*Derb.*]. |
| Tittenley | 1837-95: Market Drayton (Moreton Say); from 1895: in *Salop* [1895-1935: Market Drayton; 1935-70: Whitchurch, from 1970: North Shropshire]. |
| Tiverton | 1837-92: Nantwich (Bunbury); 1892-1937: Chester (Tattenhall); 1937-74: West Cheshire (Tarvin Rural); from 1974: Chester & Ellesmere Port. |

| | |
|---|---|
| Toft | 1837-98: Altrincham (Knutsford); 1898-1974: Bucklow (Knutsford); from 1974: Macclesfield. |
| Torkington | 1837-1900: Stockport (Hazel Grove); from 1900: see Hazel Grove cum Bramhall. |
| Trafford | See Bridge Trafford, Mickle Trafford, Wimbolds Trafford CPs. |
| Tranmere | 1837-61: Wirral (Birkenhead); 1861-98: Birkenhead (Tranmere); from 1898: see Birkenhead CP. |
| Tushingham with Grindley | 1837-53: Nantwich (Wrenbury); 1853-1937: Whitchurch (Whitchurch, Malpas); 1937-74: West Cheshire (Tarvin Rural); from 1974: Chester & Ellesmere Port. |
| Twemlow | 1837-1937: Congleton (Church Hulme); 1937-74: Crewe (Sandbach); 1974-88: Congleton & Crewe; from 1988: South Cheshire. |
| Tytherington | 1837-1936: Macclesfield (Bollington); from 1936: see Macclesfield, Bollington CPs. |
| Upton (nr. Macclesfield) | 1837-1936: Macclesfield (Prestbury); from 1936: see Macclesfield, Prestbury CPs. |
| Upton by Birkenhead | 1837-1933: Wirral (Woodchurch); from 1933: see Birkenhead CP. |
| Upton by Chester | 1837-69: Great Boughton (Chester Cathedral Division); 1870-1937: Chester (Great Boughton, Chester Cathedral, Chester Rural); 1937-1974: West Cheshire (Chester Castle); from 1974: Chester & Ellesmere Port. |
| Utkinton | 1837-1892: Nantwich (Bunbury); 1892-1937: Chester (Tattenhall); 1937-74: Northwich (Winsford); from 1974: Vale Royal. |
| Walgherton | 1837-1937: Nantwich (Wybunbury, Crewe, Nantwich); 1937-74: Crewe (Nantwich); 1974-88: Congleton & Crewe; from 1988: South Cheshire. |
| Wallasey | 1837-61: Wirral (Wallasey, Tranmere); 1861-1936: Birkenhead (Wallasey); 1936-74: Wallasey (Wallasey); from 1974: Wallasey [*Mers.*]. |
| Wallerscote | 1837-92: Northwich (Weaverham); from 1892: see Winnington CP. |
| Walton | 1837-1936: see Walton Superior, Walton Inferior, Acton Grange CPs; 1936-74: Runcorn (Budworth, Stockton Heath); from 1974: Warrington. |
| Walton Inferior | 1837-1936: Runcorn (Grappenhall, Daresbury, Budworth); from 1936: see Walton CP. |
| Walton Superior | 1837-1936: Runcorn (Grappenhall, Daresbury, Budworth); from 1936: see Walton CP. |

| | |
|---|---|
| Warburton | 1837-98: Altrincham (Lymm); 1898-1974: Bucklow (Lymm, Knutsford, Lymm); from 1974: Trafford [*Gtr. Man.*]. |
| Wardle | 1837-1937: Nantwich (Bunbury, Wrenbury); 1937-74: Crewe (Nantwich); 1974-88: Congleton & Crewe; from 1988: South Cheshire. |
| Warford | See Great Warford, Little Warford, Marthall cum Warford CPs. |
| Warmingham | 1837-1937: Nantwich (Wybunbury, Crewe, Haslington); 1937-74: Crewe (Crewe); 1974-88: Congleton & Crewe; from 1988: South Cheshire. |
| Waverton | 1837-69: Great Boughton (Tattenhall); 1870-1937: Chester (Tattenhall); 1937-74: West Cheshire (Tarvin Rural); from 1974: Chester & Ellesmere Port. |
| Weaver | 1837-92: Northwich (Over); from 1892: see Darnhall CP. |
| Weaverham | 1837-1937: see Weaverham cum Milton CP; 1937-74: Northwich (Northwich); from 1974: Vale Royal. |
| Weaverham cum Milton | 1837-1937: Northwich (Weaverham); from 1937: see Weaverham, Cuddington, Acton CPs. |
| Werneth | 1837-97: Stockport (Hyde); from 1897: see Compstall, Hyde CPs. |
| Wervin | 1837-69: Great Boughton (Chester Cathedral Division); 1870-1937: Chester (Great Boughton, Chester Cathedral, Chester Rural); 1937-1974: West Cheshire (Chester Castle); from 1974: Chester & Ellesmere Port. |
| West Kirby | 1837-94: Wirral (Woodchurch); from 1894: see Hoylake cum West Kirby CP. |
| Weston (nr. Crewe) | 1837-1937: Nantwich (Wybunbury, Crewe, Haslington); 1937-74: Crewe (Crewe); 1974-88: Congleton & Crewe; from 1988: South Cheshire. |
| Weston (nr. Runcorn) | 1837-1936: Runcorn (Runcorn); from 1936: see Runcorn CP. |
| Wettenhall | 1837-1937: Nantwich (Bunbury, Wrenbury); 1937-74: Crewe (Nantwich); 1974-88: Congleton & Crewe; from 1988: South Cheshire. |
| Wharton | 1837-1936: Northwich (Over); from 1936: see Winsford, Bostock CPs. |
| Whatcroft | 1837-1974: Northwich (Middlewich, Winsford); from 1974: Chester & Ellesmere Port. |
| Wheelock | 1837-1936: Congleton (Sandbach); from 1936: see Sandbach, Haslington CP. |
| Whitby | 1837-1911: Wirral (Eastham); from 1911: see Ellesmere Port CP. |

| | |
|---|---|
| Whitley | 1837-1936: see Higher Whitley, Lower Whitley CPs; from 1936: Runcorn (Budworth, Stockton Heath); from 1974: see Vale Royal. |
| Wigland | 1837-53: Wrexham (Malpas); 1853-1937: Whitchurch (Whitchurch, Malpas); 1937-74: West Cheshire (Tarvin Rural); from 1974: Chester & Ellesmere Port. |
| Wildboarclough | 1837-1974: Macclesfield (Sutton, Gawsworth, Macclesfield, Macclesfield Rural); from 1974: Macclesfield. |
| Willaston (nr. Crewe) | 1837-1937: Nantwich (Wybunbury, Crewe, Nantwich); 1937-74: Crewe (Nantwich); 1974-88: Congleton & Crewe; from 1988: South Cheshire. |
| Willaston (nr. Neston) | 1837-1974: Wirral (Neston, West Wirral); from 1974: Chester & Ellesmere Port. |
| Willington | 1837-69: Great Boughton (Tattenhall); 1870-1937: Chester (Tattenhall); 1937-74: West Cheshire (Tarvin Rural); from 1974: Chester & Ellesmere Port. |
| Wilmslow | 1837-94: see Bollin Fee, Pownall Fee, Fulshaw CPs; 1894-98: Altrincham (Wilmslow); 1898-1974: Bucklow (Wilmslow); from 1974: Macclesfield. |
| Wimboldsley | 1837-1974: Northwich (Over, Winsford); from 1974: Vale Royal. |
| Wimbolds Trafford | 1837-69: Great Boughton (Chester Cathedral Division); 1870-1937: Chester (Great Boughton, Chester Cathedral, Chester Rural); 1937-1974: West Cheshire (Chester Castle); from 1974: Chester & Ellesmere Port. |
| Wincham | 1837-1974: Northwich (Northwich); from 1974: Vale Royal. |
| Wincle | 1837-1974: Macclesfield (Sutton, Macclesfield, Macclesfield Rural); from 1974: Macclesfield. |
| Winnington | 1837-1936: Northwich (Northwich); from 1936: see Northwich. |
| Winsford | 1837-1936: see Over, Wharton, Clive, Stanthorne, Marton and Darnhall CPs; 1936-74: Northwich (Over, Winsford); from 1974: Vale Royal. |
| Wirswall | 1837-53: Nantwich (Wrenbury); 1853-1937: Whitchurch (Whitchurch); 1937-74: West Cheshire (Crewe); 1974-88: Congleton & Crewe; from 1988: South Cheshire. |
| Wistaston | 1837-1937: Nantwich (Wybunbury, Crewe, Haslington); 1937-74: Crewe (Crewe); 1974-88: Congleton & Crewe; from 1988: South Cheshire. |
| Withington | 1837-1936: see Lower Withington, Old Withington CPs; 1936-74: Macclesfield (Alderley, Macclesfield, Macclesfield Rural); from 1974: Macclesfield. |

| | |
|---|---|
| Witton cum Twambrooks | 1837-94: Northwich (Northwich); from 1894: see Northwich CP. |
| Woodbank | 1837-69: Great Boughton (Hawarden); 1870-1937: Chester (Hawarden, Chester Castle, Chester Rural); 1937-74: West Cheshire (Chester Castle); from 1974: Chester & Ellesmere Port. |
| Woodchurch | 1837-1933: Wirral (Woodchurch); from 1933: see Birkenhead CP. |
| Woodcott | 1837-1937: Nantwich (Wrenbury); 1937-74: Crewe (Nantwich); 1974-88: Congleton & Crewe; from 1988: South Cheshire. |
| Woodford | 1837-1939: Macclesfield (Prestbury, Macclesfield); from 1939: see Hazel Grove cum Bramhall CP. |
| Woolstanwood | 1837-1937: Nantwich (Nantwich, Crewe, Haslington); 1937-74: Crewe (Crewe); 1974-88: Congleton & Crewe; from 1988: South Cheshire. |
| Worleston | 1837-1937: Nantwich (Nantwich); 1937-74: Crewe (Nantwich); 1974-88: Congleton & Crewe; from 1988: South Cheshire. |
| Worth | 1837-80: Macclesfield (Prestbury); from 1880: see Poynton with Worth CP. |
| Wrenbury cum Frith | 1837-1937: Nantwich (Wrenbury); 1937-74: Crewe (Nantwich); 1974-88: Congleton & Crewe; from 1988: South Cheshire. |
| Wybunbury | 1837-1937: Nantwich (Wybunbury, Crewe, Nantwich); 1937-74: Crewe (Nantwich); 1974-88: Congleton & Crewe; from 1988: South Cheshire. |
| Wychough | 1837-53: Wrexham (Malpas); 1853-1937: Whitchurch (Whitchurch, Malpas); 1937-74: West Cheshire (Tarvin Rural); from 1974: Chester & Ellesmere Port. |
| Yeardsley cum Whaley | 1837-1936: Macclesfield (Rainow, Bollington); from 1936: see Whaley Bridge [*Derb.*], Disley CPs. |

**Parts of other Counties in Cheshire Registration Districts:**

| | |
|---|---|
| Aston [*Flint*] | 1837-69: Great Boughton (Hawarden); from 1870: see Hawarden CP. |
| Bannel [*Flint*] | 1837-69: Great Boughton (Hawarden); from 1870: see Hawarden CP. |
| Biddulph [*Staffs*]. | 1837-1893: Congleton (Congleton) [1893-1974: Leek; from 1974: Staffordshire Moorlands] |

| | |
|---|---|
| Bretton [*Flint*] | 1837-69: Great Boughton (Hawarden); from 1870: see Hawarden CP. |
| Broad Lane [*Flint*] | 1837-69: Great Boughton (Hawarden); from 1870: see Hawarden CP. |
| Buckley (Hawarden) [*Flint*] | 1837-97: see Hawarden CP [*Flint*]; 1897-1902: Chester (Hawarden); [1903-74: Hawarden; from 1974: Alyn & Deeside]. |
| Broughton [*Flint*] | 1837-69: Great Boughton (Hawarden); from 1870: see Hawarden CP. |
| Cuerdley [*Lancs.*], part of | [1837-1933: part of Norton CP] 1933-1937: Runcorn (Runcorn) [1937-74: Newton; from 1974: Warrington]. |
| Ewloe Town [*Flint*] | 1837-69: Great Boughton (Hawarden); from 1870: see Hawarden CP. |
| Ewloe Wood [*Flint*] | 1837-69: Great Boughton (Hawarden); from 1870: see Hawarden CP. |
| Hartington Upper Quarter [*Derb.*], part of | [1837-1936: part of Taxal CP]; 1936-37: Macclesfield (Bollington) [1937-74: Chapel-en-le-Frith; from 1974: High Peak]. |
| Hawarden [*Flint*] | 1837-69: Great Boughton (Hawarden); 1870-1902: Chester (Hawarden); [1903-74: Hawarden; from 1974: Alyn & Deeside]. |
| Heaton Norris [*Lancs.*] | 1837-1913: Stockport (Heaton Norris); from 1913: in Ches. |
| Higher Kinnerton [*Flint*] | 1837-69: Great Boughton (Hawarden); 1870-1902: Chester (Hawarden); [1903-74: Hawarden; from 1974: Alyn & Deeside]. |
| Hope [*Flint*] | [1837-71: Wrexham]; 1871-1902: Chester (Hawarden); [1903-74: Hawarden; from 1974: Alyn & Deeside]. |
| Manchester [*Lancs.*], part of | [1837-1931: see Baguley, Northenden, Northen Etchells CPs]; 1931-1936: Bucklow (Sale; Wilmslow) [1936-39: South Manchester; from 1939: Manchester]. |
| Mancott [*Flint*] | 1837-69: Great Boughton (Hawarden); from 1870: see Hawarden CP. |
| Manor & Rake [*Flint*] | 1837-69: Great Boughton (Hawarden); from 1870: see Hawarden CP. |
| Merford & Hoseley [*Flint*] | [1837-71: Wrexham]; 1871-1902: Chester (Hawarden); [1903-74: Hawarden; from 1974: Alyn & Deeside]. |
| Moor [*Flint*] | 1837-69: Great Boughton (Hawarden); from 1870: see Hawarden CP. |
| Penketh [*Lancs.*], part of | [1837-1933: parts of Acton Grange, Moore, Walton Inferior CPs] 1933-37: Runcorn (Budworth) [1937-74: Newton; from 1974: Warrington]. |
| Pentrobbin [*Flint*] | 1837-69: Great Boughton (Hawarden); from 1870: see |

| | |
|---|---|
| Reddish [*Lancs.*] | Hawarden CP. |
| | 1837-1901: Stockport (Heaton Norris); from 1901: in *Ches*. |
| Saltney [*Flint*] | 1837-69: Great Boughton (Hawarden); 1870-1902: Chester (Hawarden); [1903-74: Hawarden; from 1974: Alyn & Deeside]. |
| Sealand [*Flint*] | 1837-69: Great Boughton; 1870-94: see Hawarden CP [*Flint*]; 1894-1902: Chester (Hawarden); [1903-74: Hawarden; from 1974: Alyn & Deeside]. |
| Shotton [*Flint*] | 1837-69: Great Boughton (Hawarden); from 1870: see Hawarden CP. |
| Tryddyn [*Flint*] | [1837-71: Wrexham]; 1871-1902: Chester (Hawarden); [1903-74: Hawarden; from 1974: Alyn & Deeside]. |
| Warrington [*Lancs.*], part of | [1837-1933: part of Grappenhall CP] 1933-37: Runcorn (Budworth) [from 1937: Warrington]. |
| Whaley Bridge [*Derb.*], part of | [1837-1936: parts of Kettleshulme, Taxal, Yeardsley cum Whaley CPs]; 1936-37: Macclesfield (Bollington) [1937-74: Chapel-en-le-Frith; from 1974: High Peak]. |
| Woolston [*Lancs.*], part of | [1837-1933: part of Grappenhall CP; 1933-36: part of Woolston with Martinscroft CP; 1936-37: Runcorn (Budworth) [1937-74: Newton; from 1974: Warrington]. |
| Woolston with Martinscroft [*Lancs.*], part of | [1837-1933: part of Grappenhall CP] 1933-36: Runcorn (Budworth); from 1936: see Woolston CP. |

# ADDRESSES OF DISTRICT REGISTER OFFICES
(as of January 1996)

| | |
|---|---|
| ALYN & DEESIDE | Council Offices, 23 Glynne Way, Hawarden, Deeside, Clwyd, CH5 3NU. Tel: (01244) 531512. |
| BIRKENHEAD | Town Hall, Mortimer Street, Birkenhead, L41 5EU. Tel: 0151-647 7000, ext. 3953. |
| CHESTER & ELLESMERE PORT | Goldsmith House, Goss Street, Chester, CH1 2BG. Tel: (01244) 602668. |
| HALTON | Chapel Street, Runcorn, Cheshire, WA7 5AW. Tel: (01928) 576797. |
| HIGH PEAK | Council Offices, Hayfield Road, Chapel-en-le-Frith, SK12 6QJ. Tel: (01663) 750473. |
| MACCLESFIELD | 1 Park Street, Macclesfield, Cheshire, SK11 6SR. Tel: (01625) 423463 or 423861. |
| MANCHESTER | Elliot House, 5 Jackson's Row, Manchester, M2 5NJ. Tel: 0161 832-7692. |
| NORTH SHROPSHIRE | Council Offices, Edinburgh House, New Street, Wem, Shrewsbury, Salop, SY4 5DB. Tel: (01939) 232771, ext. 218. |
| SOUTH CHESHIRE | Delamere House, Chester Street, Crewe, Cheshire, CW1 2LL. Tel: (01270) 505106. |
| STOCKPORT | Greenhale House, Picadilly, Stockport, SK1 3DY. Tel: 0161-474 3399. |
| TAMESIDE | Town Hall, King Street, Dukinfield, Cheshire, SK16 4LA. Tel: 0161-330 1177 or 1454. |
| TRAFFORD | Town Hall, Tatton Road, Sale, Cheshire, M33 1ZF. Tel: 061-872 2101, ext. 3501. |
| VALE ROYAL | County Offices, Watling Street, Northwich, Cheshire, CW9 5ET. Tel: (01606) 815035 |

| | |
|---|---|
| WALLASEY | Town Hall, Wallasey, Merseyside, L44 8ED. Tel: 0151-691 8505. |
| WARRINGTON | Museum Street, Warrington, Cheshire, WA1 1JX. Tel: (01925) 44211 or 44212. |
| WREXHAM MAELOR | 2 Grosvenor Park Road, Wrexham, Clwyd, LL1 1DL. Tel: (01978) 265786. |

## ST CATHERINE'S HOUSE & PUBLIC RECORD OFFICE, CHANCERY LANE

Please note that both these record repositories closed in March 1997 and the records formerly held here have been transferred to:

## THE FAMILY RECORDS CENTRE
## 1 MYDDELTON STREET
## ISLINGTON
## LONDON
## EC1R 1UW.

The Centre houses principally:

1. On the ground floor: the indexes of Births, Marriages, and Deaths (from 1837), Adoptions (from 1927) and the Miscellaneous Indexes previously kept by the Office for National Statistics (incorporating the General Register Office) at St Catherine's House. (Tel.: 0181 - 233 - 9233)

2. On the first floor: microfilms of Census Returns (1841-1891), **Prerogative Court of Canterbury Wills** (to 1858), **Estate Duty Registers** (1796-1857) and Non-parochial **Registers** (to 1857) which used to be held in the PRO at Chancery Lane. (Tel.: 0181 - 392 - 5300)

Opening hours (1997):

| | |
|---|---|
| Monday, Wednesday, Friday | 9.00am - 5.00pm |
| Tuesday | 10.00am - 7.00pm |
| Thursday | 9.00am - 7.00pm |
| Saturday | 9.30am - 5.00pm |